FAITH
OF OUR
FAMILIES

W. Eugene Spears, Jr.

BROADMAN PRESS
Nashville, Tennessee

4256-44
ISBN: 0-8054-5644-9

Scripture quotations marked RSV are from the Revised Standard Version
of the Bible, copyrighted 1946, 1952, © 1971, 1973.

Dewey Decimal Classification: 306.8
Subject headings: MARRIAGE // FAMILY // MEDITATIONS
Library of Congress Catalog Card Number: 81-65395
Printed in the United States of America

Dedicated to
Lillian, Bill, Sally, Bob, and Rob
Who are my family and my best friends

Contents

Introduction

Why produce and share a new book of sermons on the Christian home? When Dr. Richard Baxter first arrived in the town of Kidderminster, England, he announced from the pulpit, "If we can lead the people of our church and the people of our city to have the family altar in their homes, then we will never have to worry about our people in the courts, in the struggles of commerce, or ultimately before the judgment bar of God." Dr. Baxter served that fellowship for twenty-seven years, and although he went to preach in different places all over the world, he would return with joy and gratitude to the pastorate and the people of Kidderminster. The pastor and people worked together to produce a church and a city that were revered everywhere because the people produced in that environment of stressing the family altar in the Christian home became genuine Christian citizens.

In the same year that one out of every three marriages in America broke up on the rocks of divorce, when either the husband or the wife was faithful in attending and participating in their church, it was then only one out of every 283 marriages that ended in the divorce court! Neither the Sunday Schools nor the day schools can counteract the home influence and environment that is provided for children. The parents have the children first and for the most hours of any other group. The "Me Generation" of the 1970s produced parents and children that became selfish, greedy, pleasure-seekers. Today as never before we need to recognize not only the supreme worth of the Christian home, but the absolute necessity of building homes that are Christian and citizens who are committed to strengthening the Christian home.

I would like to thank the congregations of the First Baptist Church of Chattanooga, Tennessee, the Emerywood Baptist Church of High Point, North Carolina, and The Baptist Church of Beaufort, Beaufort, South Carolina, for their encouragement and response to these sermons.

I am indebted to the authors whose books I have read, to the friends who have shared ideas, and to the professors who have inspired me. An effort has been made to give credit where credit is due. No claim is made to originality. I have sought to express freely and intriguingly the claims of God through his Word upon the lives of the citizens of his Kingdom to have the family altar and to build homes that are genuinely Christian.

I also wish to thank Dr. James Wesberry of Atlanta for his encouragement in this book's publication.

1
The Heart of the Christian Home
Psalm 127

An elderly but pugnacious lady took the witness stand. A young attorney with tremendous overconfidence marched up to her and asked, "Do you know me?"

The elderly lady snapped, "Of course, I know you! You're a crook! You've been a crook ever since you stole the washing off my line as a little boy, and you're a crook now!"

The young attorney was somewhat taken back, but he had the presence of mind to ask, "Do you know the attorney there on the opposing side?"

The lady replied, "Of course, I know him! He's a bigger crook than you are! He's been a crook ever since he shot the streetlights out in front of my house, and he's an even bigger crook now!"

About that time the judge leaned forward and admonished the young attorney, "If you ask her if she knows me, I'm going to hold you in contempt of court!"

In the intimate and testing relationships of growing up in a family, and growing out of a family, there are certain insights we need to know. H. C. Lindgren, in *The Art of Human Relations,* says, "The rearing of children is not an unmixed pleasure. Probably there are few other activities in life which provide such contrasting periods of joy and anxiety."[1]

In light of the Scriptures, current testimonies, and our personal experiences, most parents realize that the task of

11

building a home—not merely a house, or rearing children—not merely robots, of learning to love—not merely endure the other members of the family, this task is both problematical and promising.

What are some of the unwise relationships that can spring up between parents and children? *One of the most dangerous problems is that parents sometimes try to shift the responsibility for rearing their children to other things or to other people.* The New Yorker magazine told a story of a couple who went to call on their neighbors. They were greeted at the door by a stone-white and shaken husband and wife. "What terrible calamity has crushed you?" they asked.

Wringing their hands and looking like the world were coming to an end at any moment, the neighbors wailed, "Our television set has gone on the blink and we don't know what to do with our children!" Yes, in many homes, the television set has become the baby-sitter even while the parents are at home. What can we expect from television-taught children, reared on gunfights, violence, and comics?

Along with the problem of turning the children over to the television set in the home is the practice of parents turning over all the training of their children to day-school teachers and Sunday School teachers. Today we have perhaps the best corps of teachers in both types of schools that we have ever had, but the discipline of a child, the daily training in consideration for others and concern for doing his best, these are lessons that must be learned in the home. No matter how many courses a child may take in biology, ethics, psychology, and sociology, his first teachers are always his parents!

A second unwise relationship that can arise in the family is that some parents do not give enough time and interest to their children. It is true that every member of the family needs a little time of peace and quiet. It is equally true that every member needs to contribute some time, interest, and talents to the happiness of the family!

Have you ever seen that home where the mother is the soul of efficiency? She gets more things accomplished than a computer! But when the children come and ask her a few questions or want to pause and play a little while, she exclaims, "Janie, get out from under my feet! Can't you see I'm busy preparing cakes for my next party? Run along out in the yard and play, or go see a pal. See if you can't stay gone for about twenty-four hours!"

Have you ever observed the home where the rest ritual is performed for Dad? The hour is creeping closer for Dad to come home from work. The shades are drawn, the soft lights are turned on, the stereo is engaged, and Papa's favorite chair is prepared. The children are warned that Daddy has worked hard all day and they must be extra quiet.

Then, in marches the king! He gives his wife a little pat on the shoulder, his children a little duty kiss, and parades over to his chair.

One of the children accidentally drops a toy and out comes an atomic explosion from Papa's chair—"Quiet! Can't you kids keep quiet for a second? I've been through so much today! Looks like I could get a little peace and rest at home!" These children do not have to be told the story of "The Three Bears." They know all about a bear—he is sitting over there in Papa's chair!

Problems arise in the home when parents try to shift responsibility for the rearing of the child to others and when parents do not take the time to show interest in their children and share their delights and defeats.

Third, problems arise when children do not treat their parents with love and respect. If children make their home nothing more than a hitching post, a place to eat and sleep before they dash off someplace else, then they should not be surprised if the parents seem not to understand them. Most of the time it isn't a matter of understanding; the parents understand loud and clear. It is more a matter of approving. Children as well as their parents have the responsibility to make that home a happy home—their family a healthy family.

What every home needs most is to be a Christian home, filled with Christian love, for when it is truly Christian, the home is the nearest approximation to the kingdom of God on earth. Whether you are a father, mother, brother, or sister, the best way to build a Christian home is by sharing Christ's kind of love.

Most students of the New Testament learn to delineate the distinctive difference between *eros* and *agape. Eros* is our usual concept of love—loving the other person because of her attractiveness or because of the satisfaction the other person brings to us. *Agape,* or Christian love, is the love that forgets self in seeking the best for the other person. *Agape* is the love that builds, that forgives, that tries always to see life through the eyes of the other person. This is the kind of love that "bears all things, believes all things, hopes all things, endures all things" (1 Cor. 13:7, RSV), because this love is born in the heart of God for our hungry souls. Paul writes to the Christians in Rome, "For scarcely for a righteous man will one die: yet peradventure for a good man some would even dare to die. But God commendeth his love toward us, in that, while we were yet sinners [while we were unworthy], Christ died for us" (Rom. 5:7-8).

Make no mistake about it, my friend, the other members

of your family may not need more food, more shelter, or more clothing, but you can be certain that they need more Christian love. Just last week at Christy's in London, they auctioned a letter that began, "Dearest beloved wife of my heart . . ." and continued with the same tenderness. It was a letter written by Wolfgang Mozart to his wife, and brought $25,500.

Try it in your own home, and you will make the thrilling discovery that when the members of the family love each other with Christian love, wrongs do not produce revenge, but forgiveness; mistakes do not draw abuse, but can be faced with a sense of humor; conflict is met in the spirit of prayer, and criticism is overcome with patience. When you honestly try to put yourself in the other person's place and seek the best for the other person, your home will have kindness, thoughtfulness, and real understanding.

A charming story was once circulated about when Professor and Mrs. Albert Einstein returned to this country from a visit to Europe. As they walked down the gangplank of the ship and were greeted by scientists and newspaper reporters, one said, "Mrs. Einstein, do you understand everything about Professor Albert's theory of relativity and theory of atomic structure?"

"No," smiled Mrs. Einstein, "I do not understand all about Albert's theories, but I do understand Albert." If you are willing to practice Christian love in your family, then you will make the amazing discovery that the miracles of tenderness, understanding, and patience are no longer miracles, but everyday treats!

It was lovely in Long Island in October. The trees were a brilliant red and gold; and in East Hampton that John Howard Payne called home, there was a crisp tang of the sea in the air. But this was Paris, not Long Island, Paris on a dull, grey day in October 1822.

John Howard Payne was far away from his family and friends, far from the rose-covered cottage in East Hampton and feeling very lonely. In spite of his success as an actor and playwright, he still missed the Christian home where he was known, loved, and understood. There, in an upper room in the Palais Royal, he began writing the words of a new song. Into it he poured all of his aching loneliness, all of his longing for the sights and sounds and understanding of home.

On the night of December 17, 1850, Jenny Lind, the "Swedish Nightingale," sang in Washington, DC, for one of the most distinguished audiences ever assembled in a concert hall in the United States. Among the notables were President Fillmore, Daniel Webster, Henry Clay, and General Scott. At the close of the concert, Daniel Webster rose and bowed to the singer in public tribute to her thrilling voice. She smiled, nodded, and turned to face a gentle, white-haired man seated obscurely in the audience. He was John Howard Payne, now sixty years old. Without taking her eyes off his face, Jenny Lind sang his song that has made him immortal:

> Let others delight 'mid new pleasures to roam,
> But give me, oh, give me, the love of my home!
> 'Mid pleasures and palaces tho' we may roam,
> Be it ever so humble, there's no place like home.

Yes, in the intimate and testing relationships of family life, because God has so loved us, "Let us love one another!"

[1]Henry Clay Lindgren, *The Art of Human Relations* (New York: Hermitage House, Inc., 1953), p. 257.

2
Better Than Gold
Mark 5:15-19

Did you read in the humorous section of the newspaper where two men were talking and one raised the question, "Which is the greatest problem in America today, ignorance or apathy?" The other man exploded, "I don't know and I don't care!"

Brigadier General Zais who had many important commands, one being the operations officer for the Joint Chiefs of Staff, said, "When I retired and moved to Beaufort, I figured that at last I had no boss to command me to do anything! I could do what I pleased when I pleased, so I decided to grow a beard—after I got my wife's permission!" Surely there are some relationships we know and we care about, and those relationships are the intriguing and inspiring relationships in our homes.

Abram Ryan touches a responsive chord in all our hearts as he sings,

> Better than gold is a peaceful home
> Where all the fireside characters come,
> The shrine of love, the heaven of life,
> Hallowed by mother or sister or wife,
> However humble the home may be,
> Or tried with sorrow by heaven's decree,
> The blessings that never were bought or sold,
> And center there, are better than gold.

Perhaps the most suggestive and best-loved word in the English language is this word, *home*. Christians use that beautiful phrase, "at home with the Lord," to describe those who rest in the last sleep. There is something so creative, so heartwarming, so comforting about being at home that we describe heaven itself as being "at home with the Lord." William Hare adds this thought, "To Adam, paradise was home. To the Christian among his descendants, home becomes a paradise."

In a world that has gotten locked in with the fleeting, the temporal, the superficial, we ought to recognize the genuine need and make an earnest effort to build real Christian homes for God. Most of us from time to time have had a part in a school play. Dr. J. Winston Pearce tells this interesting and amusing story. A certain boy had just one line in the play. He was to walk out on the stage at the right moment, grasp his side, and shout, "Oh, I've been shot!" There was only one problem—he couldn't seem to enter the excitement of the play. Time after time he would stroll across the stage and mutter in a dull, low voice. "Oh, I've been shot."

The director did all he could to get him excited—he begged him, he pled with him, but over and over again the boy walked out onto the stage, grasped his side, and stated complacently, "Oh, I've been shot."

Just after dress rehearsal, the director decided on a plan. He got a shotgun and forced some catsup, krispy cereal, and cotton down into the barrel. Then, on the night of the play, as the boy walked out onto the stage, the director fired the cereal and catsup into the boy's side, and the boy screamed, "Oh, I've been—Help! I really have been shot!"

With the divorce rate rising and the number of healthy Christian homes declining, we need to be shocked out of our apathy and lethargy into doing our part in making our homes places where God reigns, Christ rules, and the Holy Spirit refreshes and revives.

This thought is deeply rooted in God's Word. In Mark 5, we meet a man who is as modern as if we just spoke to him on Bay Street today. He was a streaker and he already had three strikes to his credit. This Gadarene man had a literal battlefield inside his heart where the good spirits and the bad spirits were waging a warfare to the death. When Jesus asked the name of these spirits, they answered, "Our name is Legion, for we are many!"

So many people today are afflicted with this same problem. Instead of being like Paul who said, "This one thing I do," young people and more mature people alike are confessing, "These many things I'm trying to do!" Innumerable interests and activities are constantly competing for our attention. Recently a man said, "I keep so stretched out today I can't find time to catch up with myself! My twin sister can't remember my birthday!"

In the Gadarene's case, Christ gave him control of his life, and sent the bad spirits into a herd of swine. Even the swine couldn't stand the inner conflict, the life-style of being tugged in all directions, so they plunged over a cliff into the sea and were drowned. After that dramatic demonstration of Jesus' power and compassion, naturally the Gadarene wanted to stay with the Master and go with him everywhere.

Christ wanted new recruits, but there was another important place that needed a witness. Christ said to him, "No, my friend, you cannot go with me on my journeys. I want you to witness in a place of equal importance. Go to your *home,* and share with your family what great things the Lord hath done for you!"

Come, my friends, and let us make decisions together. What had God done for this man and what has God done for us that we need to share with our families? One blessing is our personal encounter with Christ. There in the home where we know and are known, we have this sacred opportunity to tell by explanation and example what Christ means to us and what Christ can mean to our loved ones. We are saved so we might share our salvation with those who mean the most to us.

The greatest thing that has ever happened to us is that God in Christ Jesus has loved us enough to lay down his life on a cross to save us from our sins, and we have responded to that love by giving Christ our lives. Surely Christ is saying to each one of us, "Go home, and share with your family what a great personal encounter with Christ God has given to you."

Another blessing that God has given us and that we must carry into our homes in these days is that very uncommon commodity called common sense or clear thinking. What is the definition of horse sense? It is stable thinking.

One of the most wonderful things Christ did for this Gadarene was to straighten out his thinking, to get him to make use of his best intelligence and have convictions about God in Christ Jesus.

Next to personal salvation, one of the real blessings we can carry home from the Lord is this matter of listening and using good sense in the intimate and testing relationships between husband and wife and between parents and children. We need to learn to put ourselves in the other person's place and have the good sense to think before we speak. Dr. Fred White has on the wall of his office in Erlanger Hospital here in Chattanooga this advice, "When you're in deep water, the smart thing to do is to keep your mouth shut."

The Scottish people are noted for this practical sense and one of their favorite stories concerns a young lady and young gentleman riding on the Clyde River. As you may know, the Clyde is considered one of the great rivers of the world. It is wide and navigable all the way up from the sea to Glasgow. Some of the world's largest ships, such as the *Queen Mary* and the *Queen Elizabeth,* have been built on the Clyde.

It was a lovely night in May, and George was taking Mary to ride in a little rowboat on the Clyde River. At a very delicate moment he asked nervously, "Mary, I've been in love with you for many months and I want to ask you to marry me." "Well," smiled the levelheaded Mary, "this water is very deep, and if I said yes and you acted as you should act, we'd capsize and be drowned, so I'll have to answer no. But George, row for the shore as fast as you can and ask me again!"

A personal encounter with Christ, personal convictions, and clear thinking . . . and the third blessing the Lord asks us to carry home is the practice of constantly communing with Christ in prayer. The early Gadarene talked with Christ face to face so Christ could listen, learn his real problems, and creatively solve those problems.

We today can commune with Christ through the practice of prayer. Nothing, absolutely nothing, is more important for the health, the heart, or the happiness of your home than the prayer altar. When the family gathers together for prayer each day, then Christ becomes a welcome guest and the home becomes a genuine home of the Lord.

A recent newspaper carried this advice—"The family that

buys together, saves together." One of the sharpest statements of the twentieth century is the maxim: "The family that prays together stays together." Roger Babson claims that he has made this statement before the Chambers of Commerce in all the major cities of America and he's never been challenged—"I've not been able to find a single sound institution in the whole of America that was not founded by a person who came from a praying family."

Come and let us reason together. There is not one of us who has given Christ a fraction of the love we ought to have given him, not one of us who prays as persistently and deeply as we ought to pray, not one of us who would not be blessed and uplifted by a fresh dedication of our homes to Christ. Many families already have the wonderful practice of a moment of prayer each day in the home. If you haven't tried it, let this day be your day to begin. God speaks to each of us today as he did to the Gadarene in the long ago—"Go home, my friend, and share with your family your personal encounter with Christ, your personal convictions and clear thinking about Christ, your personal prayers to Christ. Explore the great things the Lord has done for you and will do for you in the future."

A Christian family says that after supper is family altar time in their home. Janice, a junior-high student, is their regular Scripture reader and then they share a prayer.

"We all love this time of day," adds Janice. "Sometimes it gets so quiet you can hear a pin drop. We're listening as a family to feel God's presence and to hear God speak, to let the Holy Wind of the Holy God cleanse our lives and create new hearts and new minds within us."

Go home, my friend, and share what great things God has done for you!

3
The Road to Freedom
2 Corinthians 3:17-18

I invite you to walk with me up the road—the road to freedom. You had better get your best shoes on because this road is hard. It's uphill all the way. Look at the holes in the road. The ruts are heavily worn. We in America built this road many years ago, but today it is seldom traveled. We have almost forgotten this great road—the road to freedom.

Americans have always loved freedom. Henry Van Dyke had been touring in Europe when he wrote:

> So it's home again, and home again, America for me!
> My heart is turning home again, and there I long to be,
> In the land of youth and freedom beyond the ocean bars,
> Where the air is full of sunlight, and the flag is full of stars!

Several years ago there was a meeting of schoolchildren in Madison Square Garden, New York. A native-born American arose and said, "I am an American. My father belongs to the Sons of the American Revolution, my mother, to the Colonial Dames. Staunch hearts of my ancestors beat fast at each new star in the nation's flag. Keen eyes of mine foresaw her greater glory, the sweep of her seas, the plenty of her plains, the man hives in her billion wired cities. Every drop of blood in me holds a heritage of patriotism. I am proud of my past—I am an American."

Then a foreign-born boy arose, and said, "I, too, am an American. My father was an atom of dust, my mother a straw in the wind to 'His Serene Majesty.' But then the dream came—the dream of America. Under the light of freedom's torch, the atom of dust became a man and the straw in the wind became a woman for the first time. 'See,' said my father pointing to the flag that fluttered near, 'that flag of stars and stripes is yours. It means, my sons, the hope of the world. Live for it, die for it.' And under the open sky of my newfound country I swore to do so. Every drop of blood in me will keep that vow. I am proud of my future! I am an American!"

Yes, Americans are freedom-loving people. We've taken the road to war several times, and many of our men and women have been sacrificed on the altar of destruction. But today we have little freedom. Our Declaration of Independence reads, "We hold these truths to be self-evident: that all men are created equal; that they are endowed by their Creator with certain inalienable rights; that among these are life, liberty, and the pursuit of happiness." We have gone to war to defend that declaration, and yet the road to war has not guaranteed freedom for ourselves or for our world.

We've also traveled the road to an economic experiment—an experiment that has made America the wealthiest nation in the world. In the heart of capitalism we have used that mighty panacea of all economic problems—competition. We say, "Give an individual the right to compete with another individual and your economic structure is sound. Your individual has economic freedom! Your government can guide your individuals so that you will not have recessions." But the Keynesian philosophy of economics has failed today. No matter how much money a man may accumulate and manage, he soon realizes that he does not have total freedom. The road to war and the road to wealth—neither have brought genuine freedom.

I might also point out that you do not make a man free merely by removing the chains that bind him. James Oppenheim says in his poem—

> They set the slave free, striking off his chains . . .
> Then, he was as much of a slave as ever.
>
> He was still chained to servility,
> He was still manacled to indolence and sloth,
> He was still bound by fear and superstition,
> By ignorance, suspicion, and savagery . . .
> His slavery was not in the chains,
> But in himself. . . .
>
> They can only set free men free . . .
> And there is no need of that:
> Free men set themselves free.[1]

Any nation is only as strong as its people. And the people are only as strong as the homes from which they come. The American home, my friends, is the road to freedom both as individuals and ultimately as a nation. It's time we realized that it's not the number of battles we've won; it's not how high we can pile our dollars; it's not the restraints that have been lifted; it's the type of home we build that determines our destiny; for the strength of the American home determines the strength of the American nation!

What is the worth of the solid American home? H. W. Longfellow wrote a story called Evangeline. The scene is a small New England village. Let us look in on the home of Evangeline. Very carefully, let's analyze that home. The farmer who was the most successful in the village was the father of Evangeline. He worked hard and long each day and earned his peaceful place by the fireside at night. With all of his seventy years, he was still a strong man. The earth was his desk, and neatly did his files of grain stretch out over his land. His pen was a plow and his never ceasing ink of perspiration wrote the food that kept his family healthy and happy.

One of the best-loved housewives of the village was the mother of Evangeline. Her hair didn't grow grey because she worried about her dull hometown. She was always busy in the home with the great three C's of the productive homemaker—cleaning, cooking, and creating happiness. She didn't try to keep up with the Joneses and she wasn't overly anxious about her social status. There was a genuine security in the home. The mother and father had married because they loved each other, and both had worked hard to make that love grow day by day.

Evangeline had fallen in love several years before. She had met lots of men, but with a simple, pure love she remained true to Gabriel. She didn't say she would like the boy with the most money, the one who humored her every whim. She didn't say, "Well, Gabe was a little flaky tonight, I believe I'll flirt with another boy and try to date him tomorrow night!"

Evangeline had decided deep down in her heart that Gabriel was the man for her. She loved him because she believed in him. She didn't mind showing her love day by day in the little ways that make life worth living.

Perhaps you are thinking that the people in that home were "squares" or "old fogys." They lived close to God. They kept in touch with God in Christ Jesus by daily prayer. They worked as hard as they played. They loved with the simple, but immortal, love. What is their worth? Their worth lies in the fact that upon the foundation of this type of home, America was founded! As we walk up the road to freedom, we must realize that our nation is rooted and grounded in the good American home. The road to freedom is the road that strengthens the American home.

The problem is that today the American family has been secularized to a large extent—homes of today are often committed to secular values first. The lure of the secular has caused many homes to lose the love of the Savior. In the family there has been a decline in Christian practices—grace at the table, the Bible in the home and the reading of it, regular attendance at church, the family altar. Poverty is in most every home—a poverty of religious instruction.

It would not be surprising if the child wonders why he has a home. We send him to the playground to play. We send him to school to learn how to live and to make a living. We send him to church for all of his religious instruction. We must put God and Christ Jesus into the center of our homes. The child must not miss the experience of seeing his parents worship and pray in the home. Dr. O. T. Binkley often advised, "The child is capable of religious feeling long before he is capable of religious thought." The American home of today must put the secular in the second place and put spiritual values first.

In order for any road to be repaired, the men must seek help from the highway department. The big boss must be given full control. Our road to the strong American home is sadly in need of repairs. It has many breaks and potholes in it. You can see cracks going all the way across the road where homes have been severed. Today we must go to the Great Source of strength to repair our road. We must give God full control.

The first repair God appropriates to our road is the Christian conception of marriage. The highway department appropriates the money, but the men must use that money to repair the road. God gives us this great concept of marriage, but you and I must put it into use.

It includes the five basic principles of a Christian marriage and all five of them are necessary. Think them over carefully. Number one is the principle of *monogamy*—one man and one woman. In modern America we have developed something new—a series of monogamous marriages in which people have marriage and divorce, and marriage and divorce, and marriage and divorce.

The second is the principle of *permanency*. Both persons must make a deep moral commitment to be true to each other until death. A Christian marriage is a permanent marriage. The third is the principle of *fidelity*. There is no room for a double standard in the area of fidelity. The person who is incapable of being faithful is not ready for marriage. Fidelity is an opportunity, not a duty.

The fourth is the principle of *love*. This includes the Christian kind of love where you seek to put yourself in the other person's place and seek the best for the other person. You will discover that after twenty and thirty years of marriage your love will have grown and deepened through the years. The fifth is the principle of *mutuality*. No doubt you have heard people say, "We've been married forty years and we've never had a cross word!" Even if that were true it would be a pretty dull marriage. Mutuality simply means that you do not bring a perfect person to the marriage, and therefore you can afford to be gracious with the other partner and work things out in Christian love and understanding. There must be mutual responsibility, mutual participation, and mutual fulfillment. Five basic principles of a Christian marriage and all five are necessary—monogamy, permanency, fidelity, love, and mutuality.

The road to freedom is the road to the strong American home. We have seen that our nation was founded upon the genuine American home, but that home has become dedicated to secular values and goals. Now we realize that God must be placed in the center of our homes. The first repair to our road to freedom has brought us to the Christian concept of marriage. Now God gives us the second repair for the road to freedom, the road to the strong American home. These are practical suggestions of how we, the members of the church, may strengthen the American home:

1. By an educational preparation for marriage.
2. By a more thoughtful selection of a mate.
3. By a deep moral commitment to marriage.
4. By a more intelligent and generous attitude toward children.
5. By genuine Christian living in the intimate and testing relationships of family life. In connection with this fifth suggestion, let me point out that there is no relationship between the moral exhortation of the parent and the action of the child, but there is a strong relationship between the action of the parent and the action of the child!

Put God in the center of your everyday living, and your home will grow from strength to strength. Isaiah said it, "They that wait upon the Lord shall renew their strength; they shall mount up with wings as eagles; they shall run, and not be weary; they shall walk, and not faint" (40:31).

[1]From James Dalton Morrison, ed., *Masterpieces of Religious Verse* (New York: Harper and Brothers, 1948), p. 425.

4
Compensation in the Home
Luke 14:7-14

Did you hear the man on television explode, "No wonder George Washington never told a lie! He never filled out an income tax form!"

Did you read in the newspaper where a man sent an additional $100 to the Internal Revenue Service with this statement, "I haven't been able to sleep well lately, so I'll send you this $100. If I still can't sleep, I'll send you the rest I owe you."

Recompense and compensation hit us right where we live every day in our homes. If both partners in marriage are actively involved in receiving and sharing Christ's kind of love, then the percentage more than doubles in favor of the marriage growing, lasting, and becoming more meaningful all the way through life. Even if it were not for the theory of Christ's love, the facts of Christ's kind of love prove overwhelmingly that there is something distinctive, something dynamically unique in the power of divine love.

Down through the centuries men knew about the kind of love between a man and a woman, the kind of love between parents and their children, the kind of love between friends, but Jesus announced and inaugurated a new kind of love in this tottering, hardhearted old world when he told the people about Christian love. By inception and by action, Christ's kind of love means that you try to put yourself in the other person's place and seek the best and finest for that person. You can sympathize with another person

30

when you are simply sorry or regretful that the other person has broken his leg, but you *empathize* or practice Christ's kind of love for that person when you actively go to him and become his legs to go and cook food, or his legs to go and get the medicine for him to help him be healed.

We can be sorry or regretful that other people are lost, that other people are sick, that other people are suffering, and we can actually tell them that we sympathize with their plight. But Christ's kind of love means that we are not only sympathizing with them, but that we actually pray for them, go and help them, give money to minister to them.

Here in our church, I will not perform a wedding cere-mony without first having a counseling interview with the couple wishing to be married. In that interview I discuss with them, not merely the details of marriage, but the Christian principles that are necessary to build a lasting marriage.

I say to the couple something like this, "Of course, by this time you both feel that you love each other, but to build a Christian marriage you must practice Christ's kind of love. This means that you must seek to put yourself in the other person's place and seek the best for the other person. You will find that twenty, thirty, fifty years from now, your love will have grown and deepened because you will have both grown in mutual compensation."

Here in an obscure passage, three little verses in Luke 14, we find God's principle of compensation that must be woven inevitably into the fabric of our homes. Jesus does not say that this principle is debatable; he says it is there, and it works in our lives.

Jesus, the Son of God and Son of man, advises, "When you prepare a dinner or a supper, call not necessarily your friends or kinsmen or rich neighbors lest they also invite you back to supper and recompense be made to you." That is to say, "This is a normal procedure that you invite your friends to supper and they recompense you by inviting you back to supper."

Jesus continued, "When you make a feast, call the poor, the maimed, the lame, the blind, and you will also be blessed for this, for they cannot recompense you, but you will be recompensed at the resurrection of the just."

Christ points us to the strengthening and comforting fact that here on earth there are many inequities and unfair practices. He teaches that if we are not recompensed for prayers offered, money given, good deeds done here on earth, a day is certainly coming when God will set up his kingdom or his rule over our lives, and compensation will be made. It is not merely the promise of God, it is a constant practice of God!

"Truth is stranger than fiction," and certainly no fiction writer would dare put into a book these true experiences that actually happened in Great Britain. Several years ago, a boy from London was visiting relatives out in the country section of Scotland. By midafternoon it had become very warm, and the London boy saw a large pond. Without too much thought, he slipped off his clothes and dove into the pond. When he was almost to the middle of the pond, the cold water and his cramped conditions crippled him, and he almost drowned!

He yelled and yelled for help but he thought he was lost! A country boy who was plowing the fields overheard his shouts for help and ran to the pond, dove in, and brought him back to safely. The London boy thanked his rescuer, but three days later returned to the capital city, and it seemed that the incident was forgotten.

The years passed and the time came when the boy from the country was old enough, but knew he would never have enough money to go to college. One bright day, to his total surprise, the London boy returned to the country, talked with the poor boy for a few moments, and then asked him if he had thought about college. The boy from the country admitted, "Yes, I have thought about it many times, but dismissed it because I would be unable to attend."

The boy from London assured him, "My friend, my family would love to pay the way for you to have this dream of becoming a doctor." The boy from the country was elated, entered the University of Edinburgh, attended the Royal Infirmary, and graduated with honors! One day he discovered that certain germs could not live in a mold that he had developed, and penicillin was born into this world.

Years passed and the London boy, now grown into a man, was sent to a special conference with world leaders on the island of Malta. There the London man became critically ill. Some of the medicine that the Scottish doctor had developed was rushed to his side and for the second time, Sir Alexander Fleming's efforts saved the life of Sir Winston Churchill!

It is not debatable; it is God's integral principle of the homelife that we can count on—"He who sows sparingly will also reap sparingly, and he who sows bountifully will also reap bountifully" (2 Cor. 9:6, RSV). If we sow our prayers, our empathy, and our helpful deeds for the other members of our families, we shall also reap the blessings and benefits of God! In Galatians 6 we read, "Be not deceived; God is not mocked: for whatsoever a man soweth, that shall he also reap. . . . Let us not be weary in well-doing: for in due season we shall also reap" (vv. 7-9)—in the fields, and in the intimate and testing relationships of homelife!

5
Families That Find the Way
Genesis 17:15-19

All through the Scriptures you discover this trinitarian description: "The God of Abraham, Isaac, and Jacob." "The God of Abraham, Isaac, and Jacob" omnipotent reigneth! "The God of Abraham, Isaac, and Jacob" is the one, true, and living God.

All of us are familiar with Abraham, the father of the Hebrew nation, and Jacob, the founder of the twelve Israelite tribes, but very few of us are well acquainted with Isaac. In a paraphrase of Sceva's sons we might say, "Abraham we know and Jacob we know, but who is this Isaac?" Often we have cruised over this name and commented, "Just another Old Testament character, no use losing any sleep over Brother Isaac." Suppose you had to list ten solid facts about this central patriarch—could you do it?

For most of us it would be a struggle. We could say that Isaac was Abraham's son and Jacob's father but that would be about the end of the row. And yet, the fact is that God singled out Isaac and made his name stand for one of the Hebrews' greatest men. Why? What was Isaac's claim to fame? He made one contribution that assured his place among the immortals of Israel for all times. In the strength and guidance of God, Isaac built a healthy, holy family, a family that was an inspiring example to all peoples.

Abraham constantly had strife and distress with his wives—Hagar and Sarah. Jacob was continuously in conflict with his wives—Leah and Rachel. But if marriages are

34

made in heaven, then the marriage of Isaac and Rebekah was fashioned by God himself. For over a hundred years, Isaac and Rebekah made a home that was holy, a family that was fruitful of the noblest and best before Almighty God.

The Bible records God's beautiful love story of a family that found the way. It was initiated by God and guided by God to give real health and happiness. Abraham was getting old and his favorite son remained unmarried. As is the custom in the East, the father started proceedings to find a suitable wife. Wisely, he sent one of his servants back to his old home country saying, "God will go with you and will help you select the right girl."

Taking special presents, the servant set out for the far country with no references and no names in mind. How would he be able to decide? When he arrived in the land of Abraham's birth, he prayed, "Lord, as I pause before this well, please send the lady you want my master's son to marry. When I ask her for a drink of water, if she gives me a drink and offers to water my camels also, then I will know that she is your choice."

When Rebekah came, she happily went the second mile—"Certainly you may have some water and I will be glad to water your camels, too." As she did this voluntary service, the servant bowed his head and offered a prayer of thanksgiving to God. He had found the right wife and future mother. Saint Augustine prayed to God, "If I have become your child, it is because I had an unselfish mother." Abraham Lincoln declared on the day of his inauguration, "All I am, all I ever hope to be, I owe to my Christian mother!" When Rebekah's family heard the news, they reasoned, "This event must have come from the Lord. Take Rebekah with you and may her family be blessed."

The moment Isaac laid eyes on Rebekah it was love at first sight. Without hesitation, he invited her into his mother's tent and they were married. For nearly a hundred years they literally "lived happily ever after!" It was a God-inspired, God-guided, and God-blessed marriage that became a holy family.

In our own demanding days when the American family is threatened and therefore moral living is threatened, how desperately we need to build genuine, Christian homes! Our nation was founded upon God-guided homes, but now there has come a decline in Christian practices in these homes. Prayer before meals is often skipped. Reading of the Scriptures as a family is sadly neglected. Monogamous marriages are still the only legal kind, but now people have developed something new—a series of monogamous marriages. The same people who would frown on immorality accept and even smile on one marriage right after another. It is not a theory—it is a definite fact. The strength of the American home determines the strength of American morals.

One of the bristling problems at this moment is that there is a credibility gap between the United States and other nations. Other nations doubt the basic integrity of America. Why? One reason is that they see the Hollywood productions of chaotic homelife and criminal living. They think that all American homes are on the "treadmill to oblivion." If so, they know the American nation will plunge over the precipice. The tragedy is that Hollywood has no priority on this problem—High Point has broken homes and broken lives. In a recent address at our men's breakfast, Sheriff Rumple made this shocking disclosure: "In our land of the free and home of the brave, our rate of crime has increased four times as fast as our birth rate! Every four seconds a serious crime is committed in the United States!"

But thanks be to God, there are bright rays shining out of the darkness! All is not lost and all will not be lost if we, the people, get busy! It is a great construction project and can be completed only by every one of us working together. We must get busy building vital Christian homes.

The heart of a Christian home is the family altar. *The Nashville Tennessean* carried a series of reports entitled: "What Our Religion Means to Us as a Family Today." Reporters stopped by several homes at random and asked the same question, then recorded the answers. T. E. Moore, a telephone company foreman, sat with his two sons and daughters and said, "I feel that God has given me a family, thd the least I can do is to put God in the center of our home. We want to be hooked up with God so that his power and his Spirit will be received in each of our lives!"

Dr. Roger Burrus, a physician, was born into a large family. From that home has come Christian doctors, Christian ministers, and Christian homemakers. Naturally, Dr. Burrus has continued the practice of the family altar in his own home. One of his daughters, Catherine Dale, tells what the practice has meant to her. "Dad always explains a passage of Scripture to us at the evening mealtime. Often he points out that the love we receive in our family should be passed on to others for Christ's sake. I've had the privilege of helping with the care of some blind children, and guess what happened yesterday afternoon? We always put our hands on their shoulders to guide them and keep them from falling. When I touched his shoulder, a little boy smiled and said, 'I love you 'cause you helps us so much.'"

Let us listen to the challenge of God to humble ourselves, to let the holy Wind of the holy God breathe through our homes and rededicate our lives. When we pray together as a Christian family, then the amazing miracles of tenderness, understanding, and kindness become no longer miracles but everyday treats. God's love story comes true in our homes.

6
Better Homes and Godliness
Luke 2:15-19

The boys down at the barbershop were talking and one man bragged to another, "Yes, Sir, I'm the real boss in my home." I tell my wife to hop and she hops. I tell her to stop and she stops. Just recently I had my wife down on her knees to me!"

The other guys' eyes had become enormous by this time, and the barber asked, "What did your wife say to you when she was down on her knees to you?"

"Uh, uh, she said to me, 'If you don't get out from under that bed, I'm going to whack you over the head with this broom!' "

Homelife is not always what it appears on the surface. Today as never before we need to probe deeper and discover the real interpersonal principles that will build better homes and create genuine godliness. The story is told that in the city of New York, the judge was surprised to see a certain young man brought in as a prisoner. The judge had known this boy from childhood because his dad was a leading lawyer in the city. The father's book on *The Law of Trusts* was the exhaustive and authoritative work on the subject.

The judge leaned forward and asked, "Do you remember your father—that famous father that you have now disgraced?"

"Remember him?" sighed the prisoner, "I remember him perfectly. When I went to him for advice or companionship, he would look up from his book on the law of trusts and say, 'Run along, boy, I'm too busy.' Well, my father completed his book, but he never made me into a man!"

In the book, *Leaves of Gold,* Luther Burbank gives this stinging botany lesson and family lesson when he says, "If we had paid no more attention to our plants than we have to our children, we would now be living in a jungle of weeds."

Isn't it amazing how swiftly the days become weeks, the weeks become months, the months become years; and even more amazing how swiftly the baby becomes a child, the child becomes an adolescent, and the adolescent becomes an adult! So surely and swiftly it happens, and yet within this brief span of time, God has entrusted parents with the rearing of children. This is a sacred trust, and the tiny baby hands that curl around your fingers and hold on tight as you lift the child up are asking for much more than the strength of your arms—they are asking for the keenest wisdom of your mind, the dearest love of your heart, the deepest religious devotion that you can manage, and the strongest character that you can ever give. Edgar A. Guest is correct when he says:

> The man who has a boy to train
> Has work to keep him night and day,
> There's much to him he must explain,
> And many a doubt to clear away.
> His task is one which calls for tact,
> And friendship of the finest kind,
> Because, with every word and act,
> He molds the little fellow's mind.[1]

In the long ago, God pondered over which home to choose for sending his only begotten Son into the world. There were the homes of kings and princes, the homes of slaves and paupers—but somehow God decided on a home pretty well in the middle. No doubt the first consideration God gave to that home was the kind of parents that would guide his Son. This is not to dim in any way the divine conception of our Lord or his unique divine guidance, but this is to say that God must have carefully weighed the characteristics of Mary and Joseph, and carefully selected them as the parents to rear Christ Jesus. Christ came into this world through the virgin birth, but God must have surely considered very carefully the characteristics of Mary and Joseph.

What do we know about these parents that God himself selected? What can we learn from them today? Perhaps the first characteristic is their love—their love for God, their love for each other, their love for their Temple, and their love for their children. You can be certain that God chose this home because here the parents so loved God that they loved to study God's Word and pray together in the home. The first little child's prayers that came from the lips of Jesus were sounded at his mother's knee. From both Joseph and Mary, Jesus learned the meaning of the Torah, their Bible. From them, Jesus learned the power and the peace of prayer.

Parents, one of the most tragic statements in all the world is for a child to say, "I don't know whether my parents love the Lord or not. I've never heard Dad read the Bible in our home. I've never seen Mom pray in our home." Parents, the trust of rearing your children "in the nurture and admonition of the Lord" is not a sweet, sickly sentiment—it is not idle chatter—it is a sacred trust! It is one of your God-given opportunities, and you must take advantage of the opportunity of having the family altar in your home!

God knew that Mary and Joseph loved the Lord and also

that they loved each other and their children. We make great jokes about the busy husband dashing for the door and giving his wife a little peck on the cheek as he rushes past. But we should realize when the parents show by their thoughtfulness, kindness, and affection that they love each other, the children grow into the greatest security they can ever know. Dr. Charlie Shedd says, "The greatest gift that a father can ever give his children is to love their mother." When the parents show that they genuinely love each other, it does two things—it provides the child with security and it also provides the child with the best school to prepare him for his own marriage and home. Think not for a moment, my friend, that your child will learn most about "love, courtship, and marriage" from some textbook or course in school. The place for the child to learn tenderness, thoughtfulness, and kindness, those steel beams that form the foundation of a Christian marriage, is in the intimate and testing relationships of the home.

The home in which Jesus was reared was not only characterized by the parents' love but also by the parents' chosen aloneness. No doubt Joseph and Mary felt lonely when Jesus left his boyhood home to begin his public ministry. No doubt his mother was lonely when she saw her beloved Son hanging on a cross for the sins of the world. But isn't it suggestive that the Bible records, "And Mary pondered all these things in her heart."

When the children are away at play or at school, the parents have the opportunity of pondering deeply about the quality of life in the home. Alone, the mother and father can search the standards of the homelife and ask, "How far have we come? What has been accomplished? What needs to be accomplished?" Then, when the points of weakness and the points of strength are honestly faced and weighed, the father and mother can take their deeds and their dreams to the Lord in prayer.

Love, aloneness for evaluation, and the third characteristic of this God-chosen home was that the parents were willing to sacrifice and serve the Lord.

Dr. Roy Angell shares with us this illustrative story. Today we sometimes leave out the "love mile," the second mile, and we miss something important. Here's a husband hurrying to get ready to go to work in the morning. His wife is busy washing the breakfast dishes. He finds that he has a button off his coat, and he comes to the kitchen door and says, "Honey, I've got a button off. Can you stop and sew it on?"

Why, of course, she's going to stop and sew it on, but she stops and stands still for a minute. "Your buttons can get off at the most inopportune moments! Why didn't you tell me last night it was loose?" But she dries her hands and sews it on. She fusses a little bit as she does, then throws his coat on the table, "There it is! Next time tell me when it gets loose." She goes on back to her dishwashing. Toward the end of the week, the wife says to her husband, "I had a little extra expense this week and my budget's running short. I am going to need about five dollars more." He turns around with a glare, "What in the world do you do with all that money I give you anyway?"

Let's see what the second mile would do for that home. "Honey, I've got a button off. Can you sew it on?" With a smile she dries her hands and hurries to get the needle and thread: "You know, Sweetheart, I just love to sew buttons on for you. I'll have it ready for you in just a minute!" When she is finished, she holds the coat for him, her arms go around his neck and she gives him a little hug. He goes away to work with a song in his heart thinking that she's the

grandest woman that ever lived—and she is! At the end of
the week: "Honey, I've had a little extra expense and my
budget's about five dollars short."

Out comes his wallet and he exclaims, "I don't see how in
the world you make money stretch as far as you do! Here's
ten dollars instead of *five!*"

You may laugh at this imaginative story, but, oh, the difference it would make in the atmosphere of our homes if
the people in them would do a little more than is expected
of them, if they were just a little kinder, and just a little nicer
than anybody has a right to expect of them. The parents
would surround the home with an extra portion of Christ's
kind of love, and the children would grow up in an atmosphere of bubbling joy and goodwill!

In the first chapter of Luke, Mary is told some incredible
news. The angel says that she is to be the mother of a son,
and that son is to be the Son of God! By all the evidence
and by all the logic, it sounded impossible! But Mary knew
that all things were possible with God, and so she responded with those beautiful and inspiring words of faith,
"Be it unto me according to thy Word."

As parents, the primary problem is not in knowing what it
takes to be Christian parents—love, aloneness for evaluation, and willingness to sacrifice; not in knowing what
makes a family altar—prayer, Bible study! The trouble
comes in doing what we know Christ would have us do. In
the *Merchant of Venice* by William Shakespeare, Portia
makes this keen observation, "If to do were as easy as to
know what were good to do, chapels would be churches
and poor mens' cottages princes' palaces!" Parents can
bequeath to their children in a will houses, lands, money,
but they will all mean nothing unless parents build into their

children's lives the principles of Christ by practicing those principles daily in the home!

It is healthy, wholesome, and necessary for us to keep before us constantly the question: "Is our home the kind of home God would choose for the rearing of his only begotten Son?"

[1]From *Leaves of Gold,* Clyde Francis Lytle, editor (Allentown, PA: Coslett Co., 1949), p. 88.

7
Insights into the Stages of Family Life
1 Timothy 5:1-8

Recently, the president of an American industry said, "With the population growth and the technological advances of today, people must learn to be careful about getting on each other's nerves. We must learn kindness and consideration for others, and the place to learn them is in our homes." Here in our Scripture for today we read in 1 Timothy 5:4, "If any widow have children or nephews, let them learn first to shew piety at home, and to requite their parents: for that is good and acceptable before God." Dr. Evelyn Duval in her lecture on "What's Next for Christian Families?" maintains that there are eight predictable stages for the family in our day. We want to consider these stages carefully and gain insights into how to grow through them.

For about the first two years before they have children, there is the beginning family. During these years, the husband and wife learn to be religious and economic partners. They are going through a time of adjustment in being together.

One man remarked to another, "My wife has been nursing a grouch all week." The other man asked, "Well, do you feel any better now?" Another male philosopher commented, "Most women want a man with a will of his own— made out to them!" Seriously, it always takes a willingness to adjust on the part of both partners if the marriage is to be built on a sound foundation.

This is one of the reasons that I never perform a wedding

ceremony without counseling the couple and giving them a booklet with devotional thoughts for the first fifteen days of marriage. If the couple starts out reading the Bible and sharing a prayer each day from the first day of their marriage, they will build a home on a solid foundation.

The next two and one-half years is usually spent in the child-bearing stage. Three new roles now enter the home. The role of the child, the husband becoming a father, and the wife becoming a mother, and each must learn what to expect of the other. It is most important that as early as possible, the parents take their baby to church. How thankful we are for our nursery workers who take care of the children and nurture them in the love and admonition of the church. From the beginning, the child is capable of religious feeling long before he is capable of religious thought. The child is saying, "I am what I am given." The parents want to do everything for the child, and they must want to put a love for Christ and a love for Christ's church into the child's thinking and living. Here the child builds up spiritual reservoirs that will lead him through the storms of life.

For the next five years the parents have preschool children. This is a rough time for everybody. There is often too little time and too little money. The parents must work to keep their love relationship and their home relationship strong. The child is saying, "I am what I imagine I will be." The little girl wants to grow up to be like Mother and the little boy wants to grow up to be like Father. Here, the parents can share stories of Jesus' childhood and stories of the parents' childhood that will inspire the children.

The next seven years are reasonably comfortable years when the children are in school. There are the crowded schedules, the running of taxis, but they are not overly anxious years. The parents feel that life is fairly well under control. The child becomes nine to twelve years old and is conscious of his separateness, his estrangement from God. These are the most important years to lead the child to give his life to Christ and unite with the Christian family of the church. Of course, there are some who respond earlier. The child is saying, "I am what I learn." His world is enlarging and he is in a creative and receptive mood. If you do not want it in your child's life, don't put it in at this stage. For example, it is wise not to have whiskey sitting around or showing any other bad habits to the children because they will pick them up at this stage.

Then there comes the six years of living with adolescents. The parents face the dilemma of helping the child adjust when the child thinks he knows it all. I once heard this comment, "It is a blessing that the Lord gives us twelve years to learn to love our children before they become teenagers!" The fifteen-year-old girl is so critical of herself and her mother. The sixteen-year-old boy thinks that Dad is the most stupid guy in town. There is so much vitality and so little wisdom. A young man of twenty-one commented, "Isn't it amazing how much my old man has learned in the last five years!" It is important to remember that the teenager wants and needs the parents to set limits. He may kick against the traces, but he builds up a solid character and will later thank his parents.

It is most important that the parents bring their children to church and insist that they stay there, because the church gives a consensus on morals in Sunday School and Church Training, in the Youth choir, and in the youth participation and activities. Here the young people can pray together and seek Christian answers to their natural questions.

In the sixth stage there is the launching period. The children go away to college, or to military service, or get married. Here you have the high financial costs of helping the children through college and getting established. If the parents have insisted that the children be active in the church and the parents themselves are active in the church, then the children may drift away temporarily, but they will return to the church and build into their lives Christian principles and practices.

The middle years, the dozen years or so before retirement, form the time when the parents are very vigorous— they are running their own and everybody else's business. This is the time when the husband and wife are very active in clubs as well as the church. They can be very effective in church in witnessing and enlisting others.

Finally, there comes the golden years, the golden harvesttime. This is the time to enjoy the fruits of achievement. This is the time the husband and wife rediscover each other in terms of tenderness and mutual interdependence. They renew their faith in Christ because now they know from personal experience that personal commitment to Christ, personal practicing of Christ's principles, and personal involvement in the Christian family of the church are the values that they have counted on through the years, and the values that will enrich their lives and will count beyond the sunset and beyond the night! Isaiah 40:30-31 reads, "Even youths shall faint and be weary, and young men shall fall exhausted; but they who wait for the Lord shall renew their strength, they shall mount up with wings like eagles, they shall run and not be weary, they shall walk and not faint" (RSV).

8
Tips on Treating Parents
Ecclesiastes 12:1-5

In 1837 the following rules were enforced at Mount Holyoke College: "No young lady shall become a member of Mount Holyoke Seminary who cannot kindle a fire, wash potatoes, repeat the multiplication table and at least two thirds of the Shorter Catechism. Every member of this school shall walk a mile a day unless an earthquake or some other calamity prevent. (They have never had an earthquake in the location of this college.) No young lady shall devote more than an hour a day to miscellaneous reading. No young lady is expected to have gentlemen acquaintances unless they are returned missionaries or ministers!"

We chuckle a little at these requirements made of young ladies in 1837, but the same kind of requirements are made year after year. When I was on a training cruise on a destroyer in the North Atlantic, the lieutenant who conducted the Sunday devotional said that he was disinherited by his family because of the disgrace he had brought upon them. What was his heinous crime? One afternoon in New Orleans he had taken his girl to see the circus!

Dr. Sydnor Stealey's father was disinherited by his family in Oklahoma because his father attended The Southern Baptist Theological Seminary!

Today, all people might not lift an eyelid if a young lady failed to walk a mile a day or had "gentlemen acquaintances" other than returned missionaries. All people might not lose a great deal of sleep if a young man dared to take his girl to the circus. Times have changed, and in God's plan, times will continue to change. It is not always a matter of lifting restraints. Sometimes people add on more restraints or make the existing restraints more binding. The wise Christian tries to distinguish between the shifting patterns and that which is eternal. Parents need to set limits for teenagers and teenagers need to learn to live within those limits, for thereby they grow in Christian character. Christian children today need to return continually to that Book which, like its Author, is the same yesterday, today, and forever. What are some of the words of advice that God gives to his children? Perhaps the first and one of the most important words is found in Ecclesiastes 12: "Remember now thy Creator in the days of thy youth" (v. 1). "Fear God, and keep his commandments: for this is the whole duty of man" (v. 13).

One of the greatest tragedies of the world is for a boy or girl to grow into adulthood and still not know Jesus Christ as his personal Savior.

There is not only the imminent danger that the adult might die suddenly and be eternally lost. There is also the enormous loss of the years that the person could have enjoyed in the glorious and victorious service of Christ. One man expressed it this way: "When you live a major part of your life for yourself and then give your life to Christ, it's like eating the major part of a big red apple, and then giving just the core to your friend."

The first suggestion that God gives to children is, "Remember now [not tomorrow, not in future years, but remember now] thy Creator in the days of thy youth." This same Jesus, the winsome Son of God, confronts you and challenges you as he did those other children in the long ago. "Whosoever cometh unto me, I will in no wise cast out!" . . . (and again) "Whosoever believeth in me shall have eternal life!" Christ wants to save you from your sins and make you a child of the King right now. He can do it if you will trust him with your life now.

The second suggestion comes to the heart of the home relationships. In the Old Testament it takes this form: "My son, hear the instruction of thy father, and forsake not the law of thy mother" (Prov. 1:8). And again, "My son, forget not my law; but let thine heart keep my commandments" (3:1). In the New Testament God says plainly in Ephesians 6:1, "Children, obey your parents in the Lord: for this is right," and Colossians 3:20, "Children, obey your parents in all things: for this is well pleasing unto the Lord."

In conferences with young people across our southland this question inevitably arises: "How can we as children get along with our parents?" Sometimes it is expressed a little more sharply by the boy or girl with the long face who sighs, "The trouble with parents is that by the time we get them, they're too old and set in their ways for us to change them!"

This question underlies such problems as when is a girl old enough to start dating, and when is a boy old enough to forget about mowing the lawn? How much should a boy or girl's allowance be? How much time should be put in hitting the books? Underneath it all lies this basic question: What should be the relationship between parents and their children?

Homer, in *The Odyssey*, advises, "It is a wise child who knows his father and obeys him." God's Word says plainly, "Children, obey your parents in the Lord: for this is right" (Eph. 6:1). Children are not to be in awe and fear of their parents so that there is no comradeship, but the wisest and happiest children obey their parents.

A corollary is this question. A child asks sincerely, "How

can I get my parents to trust me?" The answer is so simple it is often not practiced. The way to get your parents to trust you is to act trustworthy. Be careful to build up a feeling of trust and confidence by the decisions you make and the deeds you do, and your parents will naturally trust you more.

For example, if your parents agree that you should be at home by a certain time, then do your best to be there. A certain doctor reports that as a boy he was told to be home by the time the sun went down. He thought "the old folks" were kidding, so he stayed out later on purpose. That night he slipped into bed without speaking to a soul, and he chuckled to himself under the covers, "Guess I showed the folks who's boss!"

Soon the door opened, and there stood his dad quietly taking off his belt. Now it wasn't this boy's personality that the father warped—it was a certain part of his anatomy that the father warmed. After this warming, the boy learned to obey, and because of his regular obedience, his parents came to trust him completely.

Remembering your Creator and giving Christ your life, willingly giving obedience, and God gives a third suggestion for the children of the family. This one is repeated throughout the Scriptures. "Honor thy father and thy mother, that thy days may be long upon the earth."

My friend, think of the love, kindness, and care that your parents have given you for years. They have given you food, shelter, clothing—for years they have comforted you in distress, cared for you in sickness and in health, shared with you in your victories and defeats. If you lived a thousand years, you could never repay them for the love they have graciously given you, and they do not wish to be repaid. But by the life you live daily, by your love for God, by

your love for Christ and Christ's church, you can bring hon-
or to your parents. God says, "Honor your father and
mother," and you'll have a life that is well pleasing to both
God and man!

9
Winning the Family
Ephesians 5:31—6:4

Sam Levenson, in his book, *You Don't Have to Be in Who's Who to Know What's What,* shares with us some current comments concerning the family. "Give your husband enough rope and he'll want to skip." And, "Give a child an inch and he'll think he's a ruler." And, "Be a father to your children. If they want an entertainer let them hire one." And, "What a boy needs is a father, not an accomplice."[1]

Something needs to be done about the family in these days, and one positive approach is to seek to win the members of the family to Christ. A clinical psychologist said to a group of student chaplains, "If I could get my patients to give their lives to Christ, then their marital problems, physical problems, and spiritual problems would be well on the way to being solved."

Sometime ago a church witnessed an unusual event. The parents of an American youth, Edward Gomez, received on behalf of their son the highest military award our country can bestow, the Congressional Medal of Honor.

This young man had been a private in the Marine Corps. One September day in Korea his machine gun squad was under heavy fire from three automatic weapons. Gomez lobbed a grenade into their center and yelled, "Forward, men!" As his squad moved into the heavier fire, it began to waver, but Gomez yelled, "If Third Section Marine Guns can't take this molehill, nobody can!"

The line straightened and the men reached the crest. As Gomez kept the enemy off with rifle fire, his crew set up its machine gun. Suddenly a grenade landed beside them, threatening the entire operation. Shouting a warming to the others, Gomez grabbed the grenade and fell on it. His body took the full shock of the explosion. For his faith and bravery and daring, his parents received on his behalf the Congressional Medal of Honor.

Among his personal effects, the mother of this American boy found a little note written in premonition of what might happen to him, a testament to the faith and courage of American youth. "I am not sorry I died," he wrote, "because I died fighting for my beloved country . . . I am very proud to have done what little I have done to keep my honor free. Be proud of me, Mother, because even though I am scared now, I know what I am doing is worth it. Tell Dad I died like the man he wanted me to be . . . and the kids, remind them of me once in a while. And never forget, kids, fight for what you believe in; that's what I'm fighting for."

This letter tells many things about the home of Edward Gomez—the high ideals of the parents for their children, "Mother, I'm doing something worthwhile; tell Dad I died like the man he wanted me to be." The strong ties of family love, . . . "Folks, remind my brothers and sisters of me, keep the fires of family devotion always aflame in the hearts of my loved ones," and the most obvious of all, the mountain-moving, death-defying power of a real faith . . . "I'm fighting for what I believe in!"

Today we want to help every member of the family secure a faith that is not only worth dying for but also worth living for, a faith in Jesus Christ, the Son of man and Son of God. Today it is no longer a question of whether it is important. It is plainly a matter of life or death!

Sometime ago a man was visiting the astronomical observatory of an eastern college and he heard the "beep, beep" of a satellite for the first time. The voice of this satellite could be heard very clearly and distinctly.

That night the man could not throw off this memory. As he tossed and turned in his sleep, he still heard the "beep, beep" of the satellite. He thought about how many satellites are spinning around our world in outer space and bouncing back television messages to different parts of this planet. Then it seemed that he could hear this satellite saying specifically, "Listen world, the time is short. The atomic bomb is a time bomb. You mortals must learn to live together or you will die together. You've discovered a way to get to outer space, but unless you discover a way to peace through the Prince of peace, the conquest of space will spark the end of the world."

Yes, today there is the danger of cosmic conflict in which world shall fight against world, nations against nations, and civilization will be destroyed. The scientists today have become our evangelists, shouting, "Wake up, work for peace, or blow up!" God, God's Word, and God's Son are crying, "Get right with God, trust in his only begotten Son today, for there may be no tomorrow!" Every member of every family must face the question, "What will you do with Jesus?" And remember, my friend, your answer will determine what Christ, the Son of God, will do with you!

Secondly, there is the danger not only of cosmic conflict and destruction but also the deadly danger of complacency. Father, Mother, Brother, Sister, do you really care that a member of your family is lost from Christ? My friend, do you care about the fact that you've never made a public profession of faith in Christ Jesus and joined the church? Are you disturbed in the least about your eternal destiny?

Or, are you saying, "Well, I'll decide for Christ tomorrow, I'll do as I please today"?

My friend, do you realize that if you have reached just the age of accountability, and you have never given your life to Christ, then God and God's Word and God's Son say you are lost?

No one likes the word *fool*. The Bible says, "A foolish son is a grief to his father, and bitterness to her that bare him" (Prov. 17:25). And again, "The fool hath said in his heart, There is no God" (Ps. 53:1). Jesus said at the close of the Sermon on the Mount, "Every one that heareth these sayings of mine, and doeth them not, shall be likened unto a foolish man, which built his house upon the sand" (Matt. 7:26). Yes, we all associate the name "fool" with the stupid and sometimes the sinful. No one likes to be called fool.

But listen, Jesus Christ, the Great Disturber, called that complacent person a fool. Christ did not enjoy the story in the same sense that he does not enjoy seeing a person living in sin and lost from the love of the heavenly Father. It breaks Jesus' heart to see people go on day after day living in sin, headed straight for eternal death in the flaming fires of hell. God would never have left the glories of heaven and come into this world of darkness and defeat and death if Christ had not loved the lost person.

In fact, it was precisely because he did love the lost person and wanted, if necessary, to shock him out of his complacency that Jesus said he was foolish. In Luke 12, we hear the message of the Master. The ground of a certain rich man brought forth plentifully. He didn't know the meaning of a recession. He said to himself, "I haven't enough room to store all my goods. I know! I'll tear down these barns and build bigger barns. Then, I'll store all my goods and say to my soul, 'Soul, you've got it made for many years to come. You won't have to lift a finger in the future. Take your ease, man. Eat, drink, and be merry.' " His false evaluation led him to put his faith in a false security. Greed glued his eyes to his barns when sheer gratitude to God should have lifted his eyes to the stars!

But as this man lay in the lap of his superficial complacency, God said, "Thou fool, this night thy soul shall be required of thee" (Luke 12:20). And instantly, this man met his Maker!

Whether you are a father, a mother, a brother, or a sister, you know how to become a Christian. God's Word says that God so loved you that he gave his only begotten Son that if you will believe in him, you will not perish but you will have eternal life. "If thou shalt confess with thy mouth the Lord Jesus, and shalt believe in thine heart that God hath raised him from the dead, thou shalt be saved" (Rom. 10:9). Jesus Christ invites, "[He] that cometh to me I will in no wise cast out" (John 6:37).

No matter how much your family prays for you and warns you about the dangers of putting off your decision, you must decide for Christ and be found by Christ or you'll continue to be lost!

A few months ago it was my privilege to preach a sermon at Jackson, Mississippi. There they tell this astonishing true story. Between Jackson and Vicksburg there flows the Big Black River. A few years ago this river overflowed its banks in the middle of the night and washed away the bridge that connected the highway.

Two courageous men risked their lives to climb out on the wreckage in the middle of the swirling waters and warn the approaching cars to stop. These men yelled, jumped up and down, flashed their lights, waved their flags, and did everything they could to stop them: nevertheless, fifteen cars refused to heed the warning and plunged right on over the bank and into the swirling waters to the death of their passengers!

Perhaps God has been warning you for some time, calling you, loving you, seeking to lead you to Christ. Won't you give your life to Christ today? Tomorrow is always too late! Decide now to take your stand for Christ—today.

[1]Sam Levenson, *You Don't Have to Be in Who's Who to Know What's What* (New York: Pocket Books, 1979), p. 49.

10
A Violent, Mixed-up Kid
2 Samuel 14:25-28

A fly fisherman asked a little boy in amazement, "Sonny, did you catch all those bream with just worms?"

"Well," qualified the boy, "there was some brains at the other end of the pole."

One of the intriguing things about the way our brains work is that we naturally rebel against overneglect or over-protection. If a father or a mother overprotects a child, that child will ultimately rebel. As the child grows up, he must grow up in the home, and the parents have the responsibility of working with that child to see that he matures, that he also grows up out of the home and becomes an adult. Parents are not completely responsible for a child's adult actions because the child also makes choices and is responsible for his choices.

But it is amazing, simply amazing, how the overprotecting parent can affect the destiny of the child. The Bible abounds in striking pictures of mixed-up children, and perhaps the most striking picture is the story of Absalom, son of David. Second Samuel 14:25 gives us one picture of Absalom's personality. "But in all Israel there was none to be so much praised as Absalom for his beauty: from the sole of his foot even to the crown of his head there was no blemish in him."

Compare this picture with the striking contrast in 2 Samuel 18:14-15—Absalom was fleeing from his father's favorite general. As he rode under a thick oak tree, Absalom's head was caught in the limbs and his mule continued on, leaving him hanging there. Without a moment's hesitation, General Joab hurled darts into the young man's heart, and his own closest servants turned on Absalom and killed him!

In less than a year's time, Absalom went from the most handsome and the most promising man in Israel to a dead carcass hanging from a tree for the birds to devour, brutally killed by the same men who could have been his closest friends! How did it happen? What caused this catastrophe? What can we learn from this true story of Absalom?

One lesson is that the character of the parents does affect the deeds of the children. More than anything else in the world, the little boys in the family want to grow up to be like dad, and the little girls want to grow up to be like mother. In this case, David's great sins of trickery, murder, and adultery came just before Absalom's rebellion.

You remember how David looked down from the palace walls and desired Bathsheba, the wife of Uriah. David devised a tricky scheme to place Uriah at the front of his armies where he would most certainly be killed, and then David took Bathsheba and made her his own.

It's not too surprising that very soon thereafter Absalom was tricking his father, David. Absalom's brother, Amnon, raped his sister, Tamar. Out of shock and anger, Absalom devised a way to destroy his brother for this sin. Absalom asked King David, "Father, I must go on a long journey and I will need help. Let my brother Amnon go with me. He can keep me company, and he can also be near in case of danger." Not knowing what had happened among his children, David answered, "That sounds like a good plan, my boy. It's a good thing for you brothers to be together. I'm sure you will enjoy the trip."

No sooner were they out of sight of the palace than the tricky Absalom—the young man who had learned his deceit and chicanery not from another boy, not from a servant, but directly from his daddy—said to his hired murderers, "Watch us carefully as we go through that path in the mountains. We'll have to slow down and Amnon will be unprotected. Watch him closely, pounce upon him, and stab him to death!" Amnon didn't have the slightest chance, and he was brutally murdered by his own brother, Absalom.

It is one of the heaviest responsibilities that God gives, this responsibility of being parents. It is an inevitable law— little boys want to be like Father and little girls want to be like Mother. There is little or no connection between the moral exhortations of the parents and the action of the children, but there is a dynamic relationship between the *action* of the parents and the *action* of the children. Unless something radical intervenes, that little boy is going to take on both the good and the bad traits his father shows himself to have. That little girl is going to take on both the good and the bad traits that her mother shows herself to have. To be sure, the child must grow up and become an adult and make choices of his own, but the character he was led to build by his parents as a child will greatly affect the choices he makes as an adult.

The second lesson we learn from Absalom is that when the parents overprotect or spoil the child, the child does not really appreciate it. He rebels. Do you think old David wasn't crazy about his boy, Absalom? Why, little Abby was a little carbon copy of the king—intelligent, handsome, strong, and a great soldier—David must have considered Absalom a great son!

How did David treat Absalom after everybody knew he

murdered his brother in cold blood? Did David say, "My son, you have sinned. Murder is a crime against God and against your brother, and you must be punished for this sin"?

No! David didn't even cross his son, Absalom! You remember what the king said, "Well, let's keep peace in the family. No use bothering the boy, Absalom." Then the king made a pretty sure and safe rationalization. "After all, Amnon is dead. He won't argue with us."

No, dead men do not argue orally, but Amnon's blood stayed on Absalom's hands for the rest of his life, because Absalom did not repent of his sin, did not make atonement, and he too soon went the way of the sword.

What was Absalom's immediate reaction to this overprotection, this spoiling? Did he say, "Well, Dad's a pretty good guy to take care of me like that"? Not for a second! As soon as he walked out of the palace, Absalom strolled down to the main gate of the city and started his campaign to kill his own father and make himself king.

He would stop each caravan coming into the city and say, "You boys come from the south, or the west, or the east, or the north? Yeah man, I know you got problems down there. King David is too busy to bother with you but, boys, if I were king, I'd listen to your problems and help you solve them."

Tricky? Yes. Clever? Yes. Absalom turned against his own dad, and soon he raised an army and was ready to march against David and kill him. Absalom had deceived many people, and they really thought he wanted to help them, so he amassed a tremendous army.

But even then, David didn't see the light. He overprotected his boy to the end. He told his best general, "Now, Joab, get your armies together and go whip Absalom's army, but Joab, don't hurt a hair on Absalom's head. Bring him back safely."

You remember the death of Absalom. Joab and the king's men ruthlessly defeated Absalom's warriors, and Absalom fled for his life. As he was retreating, his hair was caught in an oak tree, and while he was hanging there, Joab hurled darts through his body. Then Joab's closest servants pounced upon him and killed him.

We are all familiar with the famous cry that leaped from the lips of the heartbroken David when he heard the news. "O Absalom, my Absalom, would to God that I had died for thee!" Perhaps at the end, even the doting father realized that it was not his general, not his warriors, but his overprotection that actually destroyed his son.

Two vivid and searching lessons we learn from this story of Absalom and his father. One is for better or for worse, our children want to be and will be like their parents so, the parents need to live as maximum Christians daily.

Second, we learn that we are to love, cherish, and care for our children, but when we overprotect them, when we refuse to let them grow into adults, when we spoil them, we are not loving them—we are destroying them! May God help us to learn the great principles of parenthood from his Word, and with his strength and guidance, be good, wholesome, Christian parents to our children.

11
"God-Fearing Parents"
Proverbs 22:1-6

O. K. Armstrong writes on the strength of his home. "We always read a verse of Scripture and have a prayer at mealtime. Occasionally an older boy will lead us or maybe Jimmy will thank the Lord for the hot dogs and taters we got for supper. It's usually spontaneous, and it makes us feel that God is a partner in our home."

The Scriptures start, "In the beginning, God." After these opening words, we find God creating the world, man, and the first institution—the family. It is significant that the first institution a child knows anything about is his home. Even before he learns about the church and the school, he acts and reacts in his home.

The Ten Commandments are divided into two sections. After the first section concerning God and man, the section on man and man begins, "Honour thy father and thy mother: that thy days may be long upon the land which the Lord thy God giveth thee."

This is a direct command from the living God which is not debatable. It must be obeyed to the letter. It demands that children honor their parents, and surely there is a deep sense in which all children should honor their parents. If a child tried to pay back all of the sacrifice and service his parents have showered upon him, it would be impossible. If he tried to return in dollars and cents all the parents had given him, it would be equally impossible. Every child owes honor to his parents whether he wants to give it or not. But how much more honor children will give to honorable parents! How much more love they will shower on parents who are lovable! How deeply they will respect parents who are respectable!

The greatest crime that is perpetuated against the youth of our day is the crime of parental delinquency. Too many fathers have traded honesty for shrewdness, truth for "little white lies," the gospel of greed for the gospel of Christ. Too many mothers have traded modesty for madness, charm for cosmetics, the rearing of children for the raising of cocktails. The father and mother who are too busy for family prayer are too busy! Parents that are too indifferent to win their children to Christ are too indifferent to be parents!

Ida Elizabeth Eisenhower, mother of Dwight D. Eisenhower, reared her boys to manhood believing in the Bible, faith, and prayer. One night a week the family gathered in the parlor to read the Bible. Before he was eighteen, Dwight read the Bible twice from Genesis to Revelation. He grew up with faith in Christ and a belief in the power of prayer. The former President often said, "Freedom itself means nothing unless there is faith."

One of his recent biographers writes: "It is a hackneyed phrase to say that a man was reared by 'God-fearing parents.' " But in Eisenhower's case, that is an exact statement. He well remembers the worship in his boyhood home, with his father reading from a large Bible and occasionally halting to emphasize a special text to his six sons. He recalled his mother's loving advice to him, "Dwight, do your best, and leave the rest to God."[1]

It is far more than a play on words to say that "the family that prays together, stays together!" Nothing can take the place of searching the Scriptures and sharing a prayer in the home. A certain deacon heard a sermon on the family altar and made an important decision. "We are going to read the Bible and pray in our home every day. We will start today."

When they sat down at the dinner table, the deacon told his family his decision and took out the Bible. Boldly he read a passage and paused for prayer. He had never prayed before just his wife, daughter, and son, so it was hard to get started. After a few futile attempts, the children began to snicker. The deacon was a good sport and he smiled, too. Inwardly, his heart was broken, but he resolved to try again with God's help.

At suppertime he read a passage of Scripture again, then he knelt and prayed with his family. The words flowed easily, and when he finished, his little daughter threw her arms around his neck and exclaimed, "Oh, Daddy, thank you for bringing Jesus into our home. I'm awful glad we're having family prayers!" An unknown author wrote:

> If every home were an altar
> Where harsh or angry thoughts
> Were cast aside for a kindly one,
> And true forgiveness sought,
>
> If every home were an altar
> Where hearts weighed down with care,
> Could find sustaining strength and grace
> In the sweet uplift of prayer;
>
> Then solved would be earth's problems,
> Banished sins curse and blight;
> For God's own love would radiate
> From every altar light.

Yes, as a church family, we long for many blessings to come to each person. The deepest and dearest blessing would be for every home to have a family altar. If every family in our city worshiped in the home, then hundreds more would worship in the church. The highest honor that can come to any parents is to have their children say, "Mother and Dad helped us worship at home, and they led us to Jesus Christ."

What is the right age to win a child to Christ? Is there an age when they are too young? Suppose your nine-year-old child comes to you. "Mother, I want to give my life to Christ and join the church." Are you prepared to brush his request aside, saying, "You don't understand all about being a Christian!" or, "You're much too young!"

Samuel Taylor Coleridge was one of the greatest poets in the English language. A visitor said to him, "I'm completely against religious instruction for the young people. I'll never prejudice my child in favor of any form of religion. I'll just let him decide when he's mature and can choose objectively."

The reply of Coleridge is well worth pondering. "Why prejudice a garden in favor of flowers or vegetables or fruit? Why not let the clods decide for themselves between weeds or cockleburs?"

Parents, listen today! The devil and all the demonic powers are doing their best to win the life of your precious child. They will do anything to doom him to eternal death. It is not a sham battle or a vague pretense. That child you love so dearly is either walking with Christ toward eternal life or walking with the devil in eternal death! Who are we to say a child doesn't know enough or is too young?

Rosemary was only seven years old when she attended a Canadian mission. One morning the opportunity was given for the young people to accept Christ as Savior. When the little girl came forward, her teacher was disturbed. "Perhaps you do not fully understand, Rosemary, you are so young. Maybe you had better go back to your seat."

As she walked back, her little heart seemed to break and tears trickled down her cheeks. "Mama and Papa don't want me to be a Christian, and now, my teacher doesn't want me to be one either!"

Pierced to the heart, the teacher rushed back, put her arms around those quivering shoulders, and as they prayed Rosemary entered into life abundant!

My friend, come and let us reason together. Polycarp, one of the greatest Christian martyrs whose influence has touched lives through the centuries, was converted at the age of nine. Isaac Watts, one of the greatest hymn writers in the English language, became a Christian at the age of eight. Richard Baxter, the magnificent preacher of the gospel of the Christian home, was saved at the age of six. Jonathan Edwards, the preacher considered by many scholars to be the greatest mind that America has ever produced, was saved at the age of seven!

Mothers, fathers, the greatest honor you can ever receive must come from your children. Can they sincerely say of you—"My mother and father taught me to read the Bible and worship in my home. They were the ones who led me to Jesus Christ."

[1]Morin Relman, *Dwight D. Eisenhower, a Gauge to Greatness* (New York: Simon and Schuster, 1969), p. 13.

12
Moral Stamina for the Family
Matthew 9:37-38

If we want a critical judgment on the events of history, we turn to a historian. Edward Gibbon spent most of his life studying the decline and fall of one of the greatest empires the world has ever known, the Roman Empire. After this meticulous study, the eminent historian listed at least five causes for the deterioration and downfall of Rome.

He gives them in this order:

1. Divorce, the rapid increase of which destroyed the sanctity of the home

2. Taxes, mounting higher and higher with public money spent on subsidies and celebrations

3. Pleasure, resulting in a craze for sports more exciting and more brutal every year

4. Armaments, bigger and better ways to destroy enemies without when the real enemy was within

5. Religion, becoming a mere form, lacking life, losing the respect of, and the hold on, the peoples' everyday living.

You do not have to be a historian, or to make even a cursory analysis of history, to read the signs of the times and discern that today these same faults are gnawing away at the foundation of the United States today. Several years ago, we were out of the war years and the hysteria connected with the war, and we were delighted that the divorce rate was declining in America. But today, at this very hour, the divorce rate has gone back up to one of the highest percentages in history. With the increasing demands for shorter hours per work day and a shorter work week, we are now witnessing a craze for more exciting and more brutal pleasures every year. Violence is piled upon violence! We are spending not thousands—not millions—we are spending billions of dollars to build bigger and better weapons with which to destroy our enemies and ourselves. Recently Bill Brock, then head of the Republican Party, said we in the United States could destroy the whole world seventy times over!

In the long ago, Jesus went about throughout all the cities and villages and saw the people being scattered as sheep without a shepherd. The sight of people and their acute needs always moved our Master with compassion, and surely the sight of the needs of the people of the United States today should move our hearts with compassion.

How did Jesus counsel his immediate disciples? "The harvest truly is plenteous, but the labourers are few; pray ye therefore the Lord of the harvest, that he will send forth labourers into his harvest" (Matt. 9:37). Jesus gives the early disciples and his modern disciples three unshakable and unavoidable directions—pray, repent, and take your moral stand!

Jesus declares the harvest is plenteous, the laborers are few—or here is a need, the harvest, and here's the answer to this need, the laborers. In modern-day America, with our ingrained pragmatic approach to life, when we see a need and the answer to the need, we are inclined to rush in and say, "Let's get these two together at once!" But this is not the method of our Lord. Jesus said, "Here is the harvest, and you are the laborers, therefore, begin by *praying* to the Lord God of the harvest. We shall never bring the moral awakening and the spiritual stamina that the people of

America need until we throb with power from on high, until the cataclysmic power of Almighty God pours out of the heavens and surges through our hearts and makes us more than conquerors through him that loved us! Long before we rise up for action, we must first go to our knees for prayer. After we have humbled ourselves and prayed that God's Holy Spirit will use our little lives as his divine instruments, then we shall be ready to rise up and meet people's spiritual needs.

Secondly, we need to repent of our sins. In Romans 3:23 we read, "All have sinned, and come short of the glory of God."

Dr. Will Durant, author of *The Story of Philosophy* and other effective books, gave these opinions at the age of seventy-eight: "Most of our literature and social philosophy after 1850 was the voice of freedom against authority, of a child against the parent, of the man against the state. Through many years, like many unplaced youth . . . I shared in that individual revolt . . . But now that I, too, am old, I wonder whether the battle I fought was not too completely won. Have we too much freedom? Have we so long ridiculed authority in the family, discipline in education, rules in art, decency in conduct, and law in the state that our liberation has brought us close to chaos?"[1]

Dr. Durant continues, "Should we be free to commit murder and escape punishment on the ground of 'temporary insanity'? . . . Should people be free to sell to any minor who has the price, the most obscene book of the eighteenth century while we deplore the spread of crime and unwed motherhood among our youth? . . . or, should our freedom be regulated for the common good?"[2]

You see, in the vast industrial revolution that has caught up the whole world in its blanket of indifference, the importance of each individual person has been lost or sublimated in "the man in the grey flannel suit" or the number, rather than the name, that increases production. If America is ever going to meet her divine date with destiny, we must re-emphasize the importance of each individual's responsibility under God and the possibility that each individual can make a moral and spiritual impact upon the family, the surges of society, the corporate group! You as an individual are responsible to God, and you as an individual can make a difference for God in your family. As Jesus said in the long ago, each disciple must pray, repent of his sins, and then go with the gospel of moral rightness, spiritual renewal, and exciting life in Christ Jesus!

In the ancient Roman Empire it was popular to attend the coliseum, and watch two gladiators march out into the arena, kick and sock each other until one man was left a bloody pulp in death.

One day a man named Telemachus, who had recently found new life in Christ, realized that human life was precious. As the crowd cheered and jeered two gladiators, Telemachus raced out into the center of the arena and cried, "In the name of Jesus Christ, desist from this carnage!" He pushed the two gladiators apart and tried to save their lives, but one of the emperor's guards rushed out and stabbed Telemachus in the heart.

One of the spectators in the stands, gazing on this need-less, wasteful, bloody loss, stood to his feet and quietly walked out of the coliseum. The historian records that this spectator was followed by another spectator and another and another, until finally the coliseum was "left naked in the moonlight, bare, and utterly alone!"

A modern sequel to this ancient story happened in Washington, DC. Mr. Guy H. Birdsall of Wisconsin was the head legal counsel for the Veterans Administration. One evening he and his wife and another couple went to see the much-publicized play, *The Voice of the Turtle*, that was showing at the National Theatre on Pennsylvania Avenue.

As they sat in one section of the balcony and watched the play, Mr. Birdsall turned to his wife and said, "Lillian, I'm not going to listen to these immoral ideas and this immoral language any longer." And so in the middle of the play, Guy Birdsall stood up from his seat and walked out of the theater. His wife followed close behind and then the other couple came with them. In a short while they were followed by other spectators until, by the time the play had reached the third act, an entire section of the balcony was empty, and three days later the play was closed.

Your chance may come in your home, in a schoolroom, in your place of business. Christ says to pray, repent, and let your individual witness count for him, and you will make a difference in the intimate and testing relationships of your family life, in your nation, and in your world!

[1]Will and Ariel Durant, *A Dual Autobiography* (New York: Simon and Schuster, 1977), p. 366.
[2]Ibid.

13
Christ's Way to Win the Children
John 14:12-17

The *Reader's Digest* carried this statement, "Isn't it a blessing that God gives us twelve years to learn to love our children before they become teenagers!" Most of us would agree that we are thankful for our children at every age and stage in their lives, and we want the best for them. When Dr. Gaines S. Dobbins's book, *Winning the Children*, came off the press, Dr. Sydnor Stealey made this comment, "I've known Dr. Dobbins for over thirty years, and worked side by side with him for almost as long, but this book is the finest thing he has ever done." Truly it is a great book because it stays close to Christ's ways of winning the children.

Not long ago, Howard Stein, president of the Dreyfus Fund, reported that a survey of our nation reveals that there is a generation gap between parents and their parents, or the children's grandparents, but there is very little gap between parents today and their children. Parents and their children are rapping very well today—communication literally flashes back and forth, and rapport is fairly well established.

A few years ago, some parents honestly believed the myth that juvenile delinquents came only from the homes within the lowest income bracket. Today we are at last realizing that juvenile delinquents come from the high, the middle, and the lowest income brackets, in fact, any income bracket, where the parents or the children are cold and callous and contemptuous toward the claims of Christ.

You can rear a juvenile delinquent in any home where God is not honored and Christ is not loved and the church is not attended regularly.

Some well-meaning parents start with questions like these: "How can I keep Jimmy in cool, cool jeans?" or "Where can I get Jany a crisp, sophisticated, dynamite dress?" or, "How can I get the best food instead of junk food for my children?" All of these questions are interesting and important. But, my friend, the question in which eternity is at stake is this question—"How can I lead the children to Christ?"

We can always learn from the Master. What were the principles Jesus used to win the children? First of all, Christ began right where the children were. He did not display his linguistic prowess; the Savior stuck to the simple sacred stories. He injected a point that would capture the child's imagination, and from that point, Christ brought the child to an eternal decision.

For example, a birthday makes a good point of interest at which to start. Susan has just reached her ninth birthday. She has enjoyed her party and is still playing with the presents. "Susan," her mother might say, "let's have a talk about your birthday." From the conversation about how meaningful the event is in Susan's life, her mother may turn to the third chapter of John, and read the conversation between Jesus and Nicodemus. Like Susan, Nicodemus could count several birthdays, and they all dated from the day he was born. As he came into the physical world with a physical birth, Jesus explained, so he must come into the spiritual world through a spiritual birth. How can Susan experience this spiritual birth? She can trust her life into the hands of Jesus, and he has promised to give her this experience. God's Word is clear and definite. In the Book of Acts, we find the promise, "Trust in the Lord Jesus Christ, and thou shalt be saved."

What will Susan do after her life commitment? She can come forward after the sermon and take her stand for Christ. When she joins the church, she will have the prayers, the inspiration, and the encouragement of other Christians to help her "finish the course" for God.

In this personal, prayerful way, you and I can begin where the children are and bring them along in their interest and understanding and help them make their life commitment to Christ.

A second guide in winning the child to a life commitment is to teach the child how to deal with the problem of evil. We must not get our backs up and exclaim, "Well, our little darlings can do no wrong!"

We must assure the child that giving one's life to Jesus means that one is on the right track and headed in the right direction. You may slip in the ditch, or you may willfully step out of line. But if you are a Christian, you can repent of your sin, confess it to Christ, and he will forgive you and lift you back on the right track.

Tommy had suffered an accident and was carried to the hospital. When his pastor arrived, Tommy asked, "What's the difference between me and the boy down the hall? I'm a Christian and he's not, but we are both stuck in this hospital!" The pastor pointed to two buildings outside the window. One was being constructed and the other was being torn down. "You see, Tommy," explained the pastor, "those two buildings look very much alike at the moment. One is unfinished and is being hammered, but it is going toward completion. The other is likewise unfinished and is being hammered, but it is going toward total destruction."

The glorious good news for the child and for the adult

today is that when we give our lives to Jesus we start toward completion, spiritual maturity. We may slip or we may intentionally turn on to sin, but we can confess our sins to Christ, put them away by his power, and he will build us up to his own design and delight and destiny!

What are the three guides that Christ used and we can use? First, start where your child is; second, teach your child realistically how to deal with evil, and third, seek the response of love. Love gives birth to love. The child must understand Christ's love for him and feel the surge of loyalty as he takes his stand for Jesus!

"How may I know I love Jesus?" little Tony asked his mother. "Well, how do you know you love me?" his mother asked in return.

"Why . . . why I know I love you because I want to be with you all the time and show you to my friends!"

"That's the way you can know that you love Jesus. You want to know him better and please him, and you want to share him with your friends."

My friend, all the forces of evil are doing everything they can to win and destroy your child. You want the best for that child you love so dearly. Will you do your part to lead him to Christ? Time and eternity are at stake! Your child's precious soul is at stake! Today can be your day to lead your child to the abundant life in Christ!

14
Better Balanced Spiritual Diets
Psalm 103:1-5

Dr. James Smith recently stated at a conference, "If all the people who have gone to sleep in church were placed end to end—they would probably sleep better!" Today as never before we need to take the time and make the effort to awaken out of our sleep and lethargy and build genuine Christian homes.

Mrs. Ellen McCall of Memphis, upon being named "Mother of the Year," said, "As the mothers go, so go the homes, and as the homes go, so does the nation go!" A pastor raised this question—"If God were choosing a home for his Son, Jesus Christ, to be born in today, would he choose your home?" Dr. G. Campbell Morgan points out that every child is born with two sets of needs, the physical and the spiritual, and these needs must be met. It is not a question of answering them or not answering them, the question is basically the quality of the answers.

Some of the physical needs must be answered with food. Today fathers and mothers are giving their children better food and better balanced diets, and therefore, their children are surpassing their parents in physical growth and health. The child also has spiritual needs and the tragic truth is that many children today grow up like weeds with little spiritual guidance, and, like weeds, they quickly wither and die. The child is going to get his spiritual needs met one way or another, and what some parents do not realize is that they are actually giving their children a religion—a vacuum packed, inferior religion.

The psychologists, the sociologists, and the theologians are correct when they maintain that inevitably parents pass on to their children the attitudes and values in which the children live and grow. Parents may give their children a *poverty* religion, centered on material possessions and measured by dollar marks, or it may be a *conceited* religion, centered on the child himself and scornful of other people. It may be an *ethical* religion, centered on obedience to law and duty; or it can be the *Christian* religion, centered on love for God and Christ Jesus and expressing itself in Christlike love and service to other people. Inevitably, parents pass on to their children their own God or gods.

Immediately you can see the tremendous weakness of parents just sending their children to Sunday School. Some parents reason, "Well, a little bit of Sunday School won't hurt the chaps and it is a handy way to get the kids out of the house"; so, Mother gets the children ready, and Father drives them to the church building and then spends the hour in his car or at home reading the newspaper.

Instead of sharing with their children in real Bible study and real Christian worship, these parents are teaching their children that Christ is like Santa Claus—OK for little children to believe in, but put aside when one becomes an adult. Instead of these children gradually learning to worship the living Christ in the home and in church, they learn from their parents to worship personal convenience! Make no mistake about it, my friend. Your children learn your real religion, not the smoke-screen religion or the masquerade religion you may think you are presenting to them. Nothing, absolutely nothing, is more important than sharing

Christ with your children and building a genuine Christian home.

In Chattanooga, we are constantly building beautiful houses, but what does it take to build a Christian home? One practice is for the family to share at least one meal together and to offer thanks to God for his blessings before the meal. And how do you start the meal? By exclaiming, "Cut light on the butter, boys, it's over a dollar a pound!" Or, "Let's rush through this meal so we can rush somewhere else!" No. The Christian family takes time to say thanks to God for all his blessings. You see, my friend, if you do not express your gratitude to God, then you are saying by your actions that God has nothing to do with the food, the clothing, the shelter, and the other needs. You are meaning that the only people who produce the food on the table were the papa and the mama who provided it. But if you are a Christian, you know that God has loved, and God has blessed, and God has caused the food to grow, that God has provided the basic necessities of life!

Yes, children and parents who gather together for at least one meal a day where grace is offered before eating, find built into their lives that deep appreciation for God and that solid rock foundation of faith that will stay with them as long as they live!

A second practical way to build a Christian home is to stress the spiritual meaning on special occasions—Mother's Day, Father's Day, birthdays, and anniversaries, the beginning and ending of the school year, the buying and moving into a house. These provide a wonderful opportunity for parents to teach their children that God is not only "in his heaven," as Robert Browning says, but also in his world and is caring for and guiding his children. If you go through these experiences without a prayer, without seeking God's help and strength, then you are teaching your children a religion of self-sufficiency, or pride in their own abilities, and of indifference to God. When you bow your head today and thank God for your wonderful mother and father, you are showing your children your gratitude for your mother and father and also recognizing God as the source of all your blessings. When you stress the spiritual meaning of special occasions, you are reminding your family of their dependence and reliance upon the living God.

Even when he was old enough to graduate from Oxford University, John Wesley recalled the Thursday nights he always spent with his mother, Susanna, in prayer and Bible study. She gave one night a week to each of her five children for prayer and talking about God. It is no wonder that when the city of Liverpool built their tremendous cathedral, they dedicated an entire stained-glass window to Susanna Wesley, a Christian mother who practiced genuine Christian concern and Christian living in the intimate and testing relationships of her family's life.

The third way to build a Christian home is for the family to participate in the church life together. In the worship services we can sit together as a family. Dr. Albert Schweitzer writes, "The most important thing is not that the child shall understand everything he hears but that he should feel something of what is sacred. The experience of seeing his parents full of devotion and feeling something of that devotion himself gives the service meaning to the child and gives him the meaning of life."

Recently a certain father said, "When I visited your church last Sunday, I felt the atmosphere of worship. I felt like really praying for the first time in weeks!" The family that worships together, works together and witnesses to the entire world. No thinking person will say it is easy to build a

Christian home. It takes the time and the efforts and the sacrifices of the mother, the father, and the children, but the living God will redeem the time, multiply the efforts, and bless the sacrifices to produce the closest approximation of heaven right here on earth—a genuine Christian family!

15
The Father to the Children
Isaiah 38:19

Isaiah 38 begins, "In those days was Hezekiah [king of Judah] sick unto death." What critical days they were for the whole of Judah! No son had been born to the king. The work of religious reform had not been consolidated. The surrounding nations were clashing in riotous revolution even as they are clashing in our world today.

In these terrifying times, Isaiah is commissioned to break the terrible news to the king. "Set your house in order, for thou shalt die, and not live."

Quickly, Hezekiah turned his head to the wall and offered a prayer: "Remember now, O Lord, I beseech thee, how I have walked before thee in truth and with a perfect heart, and have done that which is good in thy sight" (v. 3). He cannot continue. His emotions are so upsetting that he bursts into tears.

Hezekiah's claims were all true. His plea was a patriotic plea both for himself and for the nation. As king, he had received God's twin sign of favor . . . a good conscience, and peace in Israel. The future of the nation seemed to depend on an experienced leader; therefore, Hezekiah made a sincere petition to be spared.

Without a word, the prophet left the king's presence, but when he reached the midcourt of the palace, God stopped him with a message: "Go, and say to Hezekiah, 'Thus saith the Lord, . . . I have heard thy prayer, . . . behold, I will add unto thy days fifteen years" (v. 5).

Naturally, Hezekiah was thrilled with God's mercy, and in just a few years, he was blessed with a son, an heir to the throne! With all the pomp and praise of a joyful heart, the king burst into a song of thanksgiving unto God: "Behold, for peace I had great bitterness: but thou hast in love to my soul delivered it from the pit of corruption: for thou hast cast all my sins behind thy back. . . . The father to the children shall make known thy truth" (vv. 17-19).

How desperately we need this teaching today! Today, there comes the clarion call to every father—"Make God's truth known to your children!"

In our day when half of all the burglaries are committed by young people under eighteen years of age—make God's truth known to your children. In our own America where there was a major crime committed every three minutes in 1979—make God's truth known to your children. In our own United States where, in 1979, Americans spent twice as much on alcohol as on all religious, charitable, and educational agencies combined—make God's truth known to your children. In our own town where children are no better because parents act no better—make God's truth known to your children!

Children are growing either like a weed or like a rose today. The weeds just happen without any planning and they struggle to mature without proper training. The only help they receive is from the outside influences of schools and churches. On rare occasions they enjoy the nourishing food of friendship with Christians outside their home. Seldom do they experience the comradeship and the partnership of their father. Seldom do his loving arms surround their shoulders and strengthen them on the straight path. Seldom can they share their ideas and ideals with a father who listens and loves and longs to enliven. Seldom do they hear God's Word in the home, and seldom do they share in family prayer. No wonder these orphan children grow up to be warped, wasted weeds!

But thanks be to God, there are some parents who grow Christian roses. No one considers it an easy job—dangers will distress and thorns will inflict their pains. But consider the glorious reward of a healthy, wholesome child, a blessing to all mankind. Some fathers do become the companion, the guide, and the confidante of their children. In the deepest sense, some fathers are shining examples of their Heavenly Father. Through them, the child learns that God is masterful, God is moral, and God is merciful. In these homes, the children mature and blossom as a radiant rose.

Hezekiah, the king, declares, "The father to the children shall make known thy truth." What is God's truth? In the king's personal experience, the power of God had been a source of strength, the love of God had been a source of salvation, and the forgiveness of God had been a source of sunshine.

Like a strong father, God had displayed his almighty power to Hezekiah. Just as the curtains of death were being drawn together, suddenly God stepped into the center and cried, "Not now! Hold back these shades of death for another fifteen years!"

Even over life and death, God makes the final decision. Today men talk of the power of the hydrogen bomb and the power of supersonic rockets, but these powers are for destruction. The child looks to his father to teach him the power of God that it may be for him a source of strength. In times of dismay, distress, and danger, this power of God can literally dwell within us and make us strong.

When God suddenly reversed this retreat of death and

made it a march of life, Hezekiah began to walk with the step of a conqueror! At the end of his course he saw the throne of the most high God, and he knew that with every step toward that throne he would be uplifted by the living God! The king could sing as every father's child can sing,

> O gift of gifts, O grace of grace
> That God should condescend
> To make my heart his dwelling place,
> And be my daily Friend!

FREDERICH LUCIAN HOSMER

The father has the privilege of teaching his child the power of God as his source of strength and the love of God as his source of salvation. In his prayer, Hezekiah declares, "Thou hast in love to my soul delivered it from the pit of corruption." Dr. M. A. Cooper of Fourth Avenue Baptist Church in Louisville, Kentucky, declared in his sermon, "He could have dangled me over the fires of hell for many years and he could never have scared me into the kingdom of God. But when my dad told me that God loved me, and that his love could lift me out of all my sins, I trusted Christ with my life."

Too many children today are floundering in the pit of disorientation and destruction. The greatest joy that any father can experience is to teach his child the love of God; to let that warm, winning, wonderful love reach down like a crane and lift the child to safety and salvation.

Constantly, we are hearing about the First Presbyterian Church, the First Methodist Church, and the First Baptist Church. But we must never forget that the first church a child knows anything about is his own home. The first pastor a child knows is his dad. The first hints of God that a child learns comes from his father. Today, every father receives a challenge straight from the living God—make known to your children the source of strength—the power of God; the source of salvation—the love of God, and third, make known to your children the source of sunshine—the forgiveness of God. Hezekiah makes this picturesque statement: "Thou hast cast all my sins behind thy back. . . . Therefore we will sing my songs . . . all the days of our life in the house of the Lord" (vv. 17-20). What a wonderful word! The living God throws his sins behind his back and remembers them no more. The life that had been shrouded in shadows suddenly steps into the streaming sunlight of God's forgiveness and bursts into a freedom song!

Fathers, on your special day, make known to your children these biblical truths: the power of God can be their source of strength, the love of God can be their source of salvation, and the forgiveness of God can be their source of sunshine!

> There are little eyes upon you,
> And they're watching night and day;
> There are little ears that quickly
> Take in every word you say;
>
> You are setting an example
> Every day in all you do,
> For the little boy who's waiting
> To grow up to be like you!
>
> AUTHOR UNKOWN

16
Woman's Lib or Let Lib
Ezekiel 16:44-48

Dr. John H. Styles, Jr., writes a description of his finest worship shrine:

> I have worshipped in chapels and churches,
> I have prayed in the busy streets;
> I have sought my God and have found Him
> Where the waves of His ocean beat.
> I have knelt in the silent forests,
> In the shade of some ancient tree,
> But the dearest of all my altars,
> Was raised at my mother's knee![1]

Mother's Day is that special time in all the year when we pause to pay tribute to our mothers. It is a time of red and white flowers, a time of self-exploration, and a time of strong sentiment. Well do our mothers deserve the love and the laudatory remarks. For some people this is also the time to demonstrate for mother's freedoms, and many sermons will be preached on "Woman's Lib or Let Lib." But this year, let's listen to a different drummer and raise a different question—How can a mother make her heart a shrine to which all the members of her family will want to come for counsel and consideration? How can mothers today not only rap with their children but gain rapport with their families? How can mothers today enrich the spiritual lives of their families?

Dr. J. M. Armstrong of Chicago says that when he rang a certain door bell one morning, it was answered by a little girl. "Is your mother at home?" "Yes, sir. "Then, may I see her for a moment?"

The little girl asked, "Are you sick?" "No." "Do you know of someone who is hurt or sick or in need?" "No." "Then, you can't see my mother right now because this is her prayer time."

At first, you may feel that this procedure was a little far out, but are you surprised that out of this home there came an outstanding Christian surgeon, a leading pastor, and an excellent foreign missionary? You see, a wife and mother who prays makes a home that is not only safe and whole-some, but also sacred and holy.

Just recently, a lady in our church said, "Pastor, you know we haven't even scratched the surface in the practice of prayer." Isn't that telling it like it is? Ask yourself the question seriously, "Have I plumbed the depths and searched the heights of prayer? Do I always prepare to tackle the task, persevere while doing the task, and praise the Lord for his blessings with the practice of prayer?"

There is no more important an instrument that a mother can use to lift her family to the throne of God's grace than the practice of daily prayer. There is absolutely no substitute for the devoted prayers of a mother for her family.

George W. Truett was one of the greatest preachers that America has ever enjoyed. People say that before he said one word from the pulpit there was something about him, a sense of spirit and mission, that made you feel, "Here is truly a man of God." Truett did not become transparently Christian by one long leap—it was a slow, hard process of discipline and growth. It must have started when he was just a boy.

One of the revealing stories that Truett tells from his boy-hood gives an insight into how his Christian development originated. He was born on a farm in North Carolina, and he was second to the youngest of five boys. George says that he and his baby brother were often left at home in the mornings while his father and the other boys went out to do the work on the farm.

Each day there would come a time when the two little boys would miss their mother. For a while they didn't give it much thought, then they became curious. "Wonder where Mama goes every morning," pondered Jimmy. "Wonder what she does?" "Let's tag along behind her and find out," suggested George.

You can imagine how two barefooted question marks in overalls eagerly watched their mother the next morning. At the regular hour, they tiptoed behind her until she had walked away from the house and out to their little apple orchard. The boys crept up behind some large bushes and watched their beloved mother go to her knees for prayer. "O God, our Father, I want to thank you for giving me these five boys. But I can never raise them right unless you give me the power of your Holy Spirit. Help me to live this day so that my family will be lifted closer to Christ."

This wife and mother was directly involved in the two most relevant activities for making religion real and powerful in her home. She was praying and she was practicing Christianity in her daily living.

Ezekiel was one of the most colorful prophets in all Israel. One day he gave the people an insight straight from the living God. Translated literally from the Hebrew, Ezekiel 16:44 reads, "As the mother lives, so is her daughter." Sociologists and psychiatrists are exactly correct when they tell us that there is no connection between the moral exhortations and pleadings of the parents and the actions of the child, but there is a vital and dynamic relationship between the actions of the parents and the actions of the children. Not many children explain their deeds by saying, "Mama told me to do it this way": but thousands explain their actions by saying, "Mama does it this way." Prayer is absolutely necessary to make your home more Christian and in that praying, there will come the inspiration and the incentive to practice Christian living. "As the mother lives, so is the daughter."

And old adage reads, "You can't fool a child," and in the realm of character, you can't. If the parents say to the children, "Run on off to bed and be sure to say your prayers," but the children never see the parents pray and never share a prayer with the parents, then the children will know how little prayer means to the parents. If the parents send their children to Sunday School without going themselves and participating themselves, then the children get the message loud and clear, that so far as the great big wonderful world is concerned, the church school is like Santa Claus—OK for little children to believe in, but put aside when one becomes an adult.

When you come with your children to Sunday School, when your children see that the Bible is not just another book to stand on the shelf, but a spiritual book to be explored in church and at home to discover God's Word for the living of today, then your children will get turned on to the truth that Jesus Christ is real and vigorous in your life, and that he can be relevant and vital in their lives.

No smoke screen religion or insincere veneer will cut it today—the challenge that comes to wives and mothers is to make religion more real and powerful in your home by praying and by practicing genuine Christian living in the intimate and testing relationships of family life.

Mothers, if you accept this difficult, but spiritually rewarding and uplifting challenge to pray and to practice real Christian living in your home, then your children will be able to sing with T. W. Fessenden:

> You painted no Madonnas
>> On chapel walls in Rome,
> But with a touch diviner
>> You lived one in your home.
>
> You wrote no lofty poems
>> That critics counted art,
> But with a nobler vision
>> You lived them in your heart.
>
> . . . .
>
> Had I the gift of Raphael,
>> Or Michelangelo,
> Oh, what a rare Madonna
>> My mother's life would show!

[1]*Masterpieces of Religious Verse*, op. cit., p. 338.

17
Singles, Marrieds, Reconstituteds, and Their Issues
1 Corinthians 7:1-5

The issue of single or wedded bliss has brought into sharper focus the differences in the way men and women and husbands and wives view themselves and their roles. Sam Levenson in *You Don't Have to Be in Who's Who to Know What's What* shares these observations: "God made Adam for practice, then He looked him over and said, 'I think I can do better than that' so He made Eve. And again, "Being a career woman is harder than being a career man. You've got to look like a lady, act like a man, and work like a dog."[1]

Without question, husbands and wives in contemporary society face crucial questions that either bind them closer together or tear them apart:

1. What is the power structure in the contemporary Christian home?

2. If the wife makes more money than the husband, should she be the boss in every major decision?

3. Where do you draw the line between major decisions and the minor decisions?

4. If both the husband and wife work, which one does which chores?

5. What should be the childrens' chores in the home?

6. Should the husband or the wife manage the checkbook?

7. Is it worth it for the mother to work outside the home and leave the children with someone else to rear them?

8. As in the contemporary movie, *Kramer Versus Kramer*, the husband imagines that he can take care of the children alone, but should he?

9. Is being single a viable Christian option for a person in contempory society? Some people choose to be single because of their career or because they do not wish to rear children.

Some people are single because their mate has died and they do not wish to remarry. Can a person choose to be single and still be a contributing Christian in today's world as Paul was in his world?

In 1 Corinthians 7:7 the apostle Paul points out that he has chosen to be single and he does not feel that there is anything wrong in being single. He suggests that those that are married and those that are single should not feel superior to the other, but that each should recognize the option as being a choice, and that each should try to grow in Christ's likeness. Dr. Herschel Hobbs in his commentary of the Sunday School lessons writes, "In singleness, both men and women can express parental love by caring for the children of others, teaching in church school, or being a 'Big Brother' or 'Big Sister' . . . ministering to unfortunate children . . . and the like. These are but a few suggestions as to how single men and women may band together in rendering service to society."[2]

One of the emotional upheavals in modern life is triggered by divorce, and one of the acute problems in contemporary society is how to be a friend and counselor to people who go through the trauma of divorce. Jim Newton has compiled a list of suggestions that will aid Christians in working with people who have been divorced. Consider them carefully:

1. Try to be loving, caring, sensitive to both parties. Don't be judgmental.

2. Don't take sides, but neither allow yourself to be caught in the middle between two irreconcilable parties.

3. Pray for each person directly affected—husband, wife, children, parents, business associates, other church members. Let them know you are praying for them. Remember the experience is much like the grief over the death of a family member.

4. Tell the person who's getting the divorce that you realize it is a difficult decision, that times may get rougher in the future, and you want to help if they need to share their feelings.

What does the Bible say about divorce? In Matthew 19, we find the Pharisees tempting Jesus by saying, "Is it lawful for a man to put away his wife for every cause?" Jesus answered, "Have ye not read, that he which made them at the beginning made them male and female, and said, For this cause shall a man leave father and mother, and shall cleave to his wife: and they shall be one flesh? Wherefore they are no more twain, but one flesh. What therefore God hath joined together, let not man put asunder. . . . Moses because of the hardness of your hearts suffered you to put away your wives: but from the beginning it was not so. And I [Jesus] say unto you, Whosoever shall put away his wife, except it be for fornication, and shall marry another, committeth adultery: and whoso marrieth her which is put away doth commit adultery" (vv. 4-9). In Mark 10:11-12, the recorder leaves out the words, "except for fornication," and makes the marriage vow even more binding.

Certainly, there is no question that Jesus means for two Christians to commit their lives together in a Christian marriage and to intend to stay together in this permanent relationship for the whole of life. According to the latest statistics, 60 percent of the people who separate in America wish now that they had stayed together and tried to work out and solve their problems. In America, it is still a part of any lawyer's first responsibility to try to reconcile the couple before initiating divorce proceedings.

When planning to dissolve the marriage in a divorce, children involved in custody battles are often torn apart. To avoid the no-win pain of custody fights, more and more parents are turning to joint custody, sharing equal responsibility in caring for the children. Most of the time this means that the children shuttle between their parents' homes. In Houston, Texas, two brothers, ages six and nine, spend one night with their mother, the next with their father and stepmother, and alternate on weekends. This four-year-old experiment seems to be working—almost. The younger boy's nursery school report card last year found him exemplary in all ways except for one obvious confusion—he wasn't sure where he lived!

Still another problem in contempory society is how to deal with the step-population. In the May 1980, issue of the *Reader's Digest*, we find the information that the nation's swelling step-population now includes some four million stepparents and 6.5 million stepchildren under eighteen. Although people like to think that such "reconstituted" or "blended" families live in rewedded bliss, the impact of remarriage on a family, no matter how high the expectations, is second only to the crisis of divorce. Children entering a stepfamily can feel twice defeated, once for having been unable to prevent the divorce, and again for not being able to prevent the remarriage.

Sam Levenson in *You Don't Have to Be in Who's Who to Know What's What* declares, "The attitude of couples toward propagation runs from potluck parenthood to planned parenthood to panned parenthood; from ensured issue to controled issue to completely avoiding the issue!"[3] In the May 1980, issue of *Changing Times* magazine, we find this advice, "Whatever is bothering a child who doesn't get along with the other kids—whether it is a feeling of insecurity, a lack of social skills, trouble in the home, or medical problems—it's worth finding out what it is and doing something about it."

How does the Bible suggest that we solve the problems and build a solid foundation of the Christian home that will be productive of a sound and abundant life for husbands, wives, and children? We can do no better than to apprehend and appropriate Paul's message to the Ephesians: "Be ye therefore followers of God, as dear children; and walk in love, as Christ also hath loved us, and hath given himself for us. . . . See then that ye walk circumspectly, not as fools, but as wise, redeeming the time. . . . Wives, submit yourselves unto your own husbands, as unto the Lord, for the husband is the head of the wife, even as Christ is the head of the church. . . . Therefore as the church is subject unto Christ, so let the wives be to their own husbands in everything. Husbands, love your wives, even as Christ also loved the church, and gave himself for it. . . . So ought men to love their wives as their own bodies. . . . For this cause shall a man leave his father and mother, and shall be joined unto his wife, and they two shall be one flesh. . . . Children, obey your parents in the Lord: for this is right. . . . And, ye fathers, provoke not your children to wrath: but

bring them up in the nurture and admonition of the Lord"
(Eph. 5:6).

God calls us to let the husband be the head of the house
and love his wife even as Christ has loved the church and
has given himself for her. The wife ought to respect and
love her husband. Both husbands and wives are to love
with Christ's kind of love, *agape,* which means you put
yourself in the other person's place and seek the best for the
other person. If husbands and wives dare to practice this
New Testament kind of love, they will discover that through
the ten, twenty, and fifty years of marriage, their love will
grow and deepen.

Children are to grow up obeying their parents with love
and respect. Christ loved them and gave himself for them,
and they are called to love and give themselves in Christian
love for the other members of their families. The Christian
home thus becomes the nearest approximation to heaven
here on earth.

[1]Levenson, op. cit., pp. 34-38.
[2]Herschel H. Hobbs, *Studying Adult Life and Work Lessons*
(Nashville: © Convention Press of the Sunday School Board of the
Southern Baptist Convention, 1980), April, May, June 1980.
[3]Levenson, op. cit., p. 60.

18
Family Finance
(Or a Tax Collector's Change)
Luke 19:1-10

A boy living in the Bronx, New York, once sent a letter to God. In this letter he asked God to send him a hundred dollars to help buy groceries for him and his family. The letter was duly addressed and stamped, and the post office, not sure where to send it, ultimately sent it to the desk of then President Jimmy Carter.

President Carter was touched with this request and decided to send the boy five dollars. That night when the little boy said his prayer, it went something like this: "Thank you so much, God, for sending me the hundred dollars to buy groceries; but why did you decide to send it through Washington? They always keep 95 percent of our money down there!"

In these days of runaway inflation and runaway people fighting for power in Washington, we cannot help but be conscious of our deep need for new visions and new victories! Did you see where the brilliant mathematician was visiting the second-grade class and raised his question—"If I have 42 cents in one pocket and 20 cents in another pocket, what do I have?" A seven-year-old boy answered quickly, "I've got another boy's pants on!"

In these days we all feel the cruel pinch of inflation, and we need some guidance in family finances.

Many times we have been intrigued by the story of the little tax collector of Galilee. It is a human narrative with the deepest yearnings of a lonely heart, and it moves through the somber shadows to a surprising climax of sunlight. When Jesus came into his home, new insight into family finances came and a transformation came into his life. The man's name was Zacchaeus and he was a publican, a tax collector. Neither today nor yesterday do tax collectors win the Gallup Poll of popular approval! He would not have been received with open arms because of his job, but even worse, he was a Roman tax collector, a collaborationist, an instrument of the army of occupation. Then, to make matters worse, the people suspected that these Roman tax collectors extracted more money than they had to, and kept for themselves what they didn't turn over to Rome. You might call a man a robber or a rascal or a renegade, but if you really wanted to whack him in the face, you would call him a publican, a tax collector. It was a lonely, friendless, forbidden life, this life of a tax collector.

When shepherds stopped to pay taxes on their sheep, Zacchaeus would discuss with them the topics of the day. Perhaps this was the way he first heard about the Galilean carpenter called Jesus. Zacchaeus made up his mind to see Jesus and ask him a few questions. The truth of the matter was that life had become sort of dreary and dull in his home and in his business. Making money was not even fun anymore, and Zacchaeus was miserable. Few things are more tragic than to see a person who is so concerned about making money that he hasn't time to make a life!

Jesus was passing through Jericho on his way to Jerusalem and, as usual, he was the center of the crowd. As the procession made its way through the town, Zacchaeus was attracted by the noise. Some stranger said that Jesus of Nazareth was passing by so Zacchaeus joined the bustling crowd. "He must be a great man," thought Zacchaeus, "a man with wide sympathies and deep understanding. They say that he even called another tax collector named Matthew to be his disciple."

Zacchaeus quickened his step until he, too, was hurrying with the crowd. He darted down a side street and came into the main highway just ahead of the procession. As it surged past him, the crowd caught him up in its tumult and carried him forward. But Zacchaeus could not see Jesus. He stood on his tiptoes—he craned his neck to the right and to the left—he became more excited and more exasperated by the moment, but still he could not see Jesus.

There were two things that prevented his seeing the Master and these two things often encumber our views in our homes. On the one hand there was the problem of the crowd. Zacchaeus was too much in the crowd and of the crowd, in the world and of the world, to genuinely set his eyes upon Jesus.

Isn't this often our serious problem? Wordsworth was correct when he said, "The world is too much with us, late and soon, getting and spending, we lay waste our powers!" Yes, too many times we become so engrossed in our work, in our winnings, and in our recreation that they crowd out our participation in Christ's efforts, Christ's concerns! Too many homes today are devoted to secular values and secular pursuits, and the family neglects spiritual values and spiritual pursuits. Too many husbands and wives are committed to this world and the things of this world rather than committing their lives to Christ and his healthy way of living.

The second problem for Zacchaeus was that he was too short of stature. In more ways than one he was a "little" man. His eyes were not on the lilies of the field or the birds of the air, but on the coins in his hand. Dr. Gaines S. Dobbins is correct when he says, "Any church of Jesus can be small, but no church of Jesus Christ can be little." We never need to have little churches or people who are "little" in our homes.

Often this materialism becomes a problem today. Sometimes people allow things to leap up and blot out their vision of Jesus. Old self-concern about self-wants makes them shrivel up into little persons. What Zacchaeus had to do was to climb above the crowd and above the barrier of self if he would ever see the Master; so, Zacchaeus climbed up into a sycamore tree. The publican felt a warm glow in his heart as he looked for Jesus. There he was . . . that must be the Christ near the center! Zacchaeus noted the kindness of Jesus' face and the strength and grace of his walk. He was intrigued with the Master just by looking at him.

Suddenly, the procession stopped. Jesus looked up and straight into the eyes of this tax collector as he said, "Zacchaeus, make haste, and come down; for to-day I must abide at thy house."

You might think this story would end with Jesus and Zacchaeus walking away from the astonished crowd. But no! There is a much more amazing and delightful conclusion. Look what happened in the dramatic events in the new Christian home!

After he had entertained Jesus in his home, Zacchaeus was completely captivated. His heart was won when he found what he was seeking, and he became a changed man. "Half of my goods I will give to the unfortunate and to everyone from whom I have taken more taxes than I should have, I will pay back four times the amount I took."

No doubt Christ smiled as he said, "Today, salvation [wholeness of life], has come to your house."

Isn't it significant that it was after Zacchaeus had decided to set his financial life in his home right that Jesus confirmed the fact of his salvation? What Zacchaeus decided to do with his money was a sure sign of what had happened inside his heart.

One of the distinguishing marks of my denomination is that every member is called a Christian. We baptize only those who can make a profession of faith for themselves. Every member of our church has declared publicly, "I give myself to Christ for life. I am a saved person."

Now how we give our money to Christ through the church is a sure sign of the genuineness of our salvation and an indication that wholeness has come to our homes. Each family needs to make financial decisions after family discussions and decisions. God says, "Bring ye all the tithes into the storehouse." One tenth of our total income should be given to Christ through his church. One penny less is cheating God and cheating the Christian himself of the blessings of giving.

In terms of family money management, the family needs to decide that the first part, or 10 percent of their income will be given on the first day of the week, Sunday, to Christ through his church. The Christian family also needs to save 10 percent of the family income and live within the remaining 80 percent of the income. This practice, the first 10 percent given to the Lord, the second 10 percent saved, and living within the remaining 80 percent requires discipline and dedication, but if you follow this practice faithfully in your family, then God is certain to bless; each member of the family is certain to grow into a healthy responsibility; and each member of the family will learn the joys and thrills of the abundant life in Christ.

Have you ever considered the benefits of being totally committed to God, of knowing deep down inside your heart that first, finally, and financially you are right with God?

Your church calls you a brother or a sister in the sacred fellowship, and welcomes you with open arms. Your church walks beside you in good times and bad, and stands as a bulwark against the world, the flesh, and the devil. Your church prays for you when you are sick and welcomes you back as a loving friend. Your church comforts you and uplifts you and lives with you every step of the way. This is God's anti-poverty program, for when you are right with God, faithful in giving your tenth to Christ through his church, then God will be faithful in caring for you and pouring out so many blessings upon you that there shall not be room enough to receive them!

Charlie Shedd, in an interview on some of the personal problems of pastors' families, declared, "One of the most exciting things Martha and I decided early in our married life was to be diligent tithers. Later, we built that to 20%, and now half our income goes into a foundation . . . to buy animals for missionaries all over the world. . . . We think that the more the pastor and his wife give in interesting and fun ways, and can talk about it to their children and their people, the more they will find their church more genuinely interested in missions. So many we know say, 'We can't afford to tithe.' But the Biblical saying is really true: 'The more we bless the more we will be blessed.' "[1]

Dr. Charles Allen, in a book on prayer, writes, "I talk a lot about tithing because it gives people an opportunity to express their faith, to show their salvation!"[2] Missionary Jane Barnette said at the age of seventy-one, "I'm thankful that I owe no debts on houses or lands, but I do owe a deep debt of love and gratitude to God for all his blessings. I will continue to pay my debt by tithing, by giving at least a tenth to Christ through my church, to show my gratitude until we all gather beyond the Jordan with singing and rejoicing in the Lord."[3]

[1]From a seminar conducted by Charlie and Martha Shedd at St. Helena's Episcopal Church, Parish House, Beaufort, SC, March 11, 1980.

[2]Charles L. Allen, *All Things Are Possible Through Prayer* (Westwood, NJ: Fleming H. Revell Co., 1958), p. 24.

[3]From a message by missionary Jane Barnette at First Baptist Church, North Augusta, SC, April 1963.

19
True Wisdom, Tested Instruction, and Tender Care
Proverbs 23:19-23

A wise old poet wrote:

> Like a hope divine in this troubled world
> Is the thought of mothers' care . . .
> Shared, it increases in richness,
> Divided, 'tis full in each part,
> For God has hidden a love like His own
> In the depths of the mother heart.

Pause and consider three blessings we have received from our mothers—true wisdom, tested instruction, and tender care.

Solomon was called "the wisest man who ever lived." Have you ever wondered why? Was it because he was born a genius? No. It was solely because he sought the wisdom of Almighty God. Listen again to Solomon's inspired advice in Proverbs 23:22-23, "Despise not thy mother when she is old. Buy the truth, and sell it not; also wisdom, and instruction, and understanding."

Where did you learn the true wisdom of the statement by Jesus—"It is more blessed to give than to receive?" Was it not from your mother's example? Certainly, it was that way for Johnny Green. Johnny was not too happy with his allowance, so he decided to show Mom just how valuable he was. As she picked up the breakfast plate one morning, his mother discovered a bill from her son. Mother owes Johnny:

1. For running three errands................$ .15
2. For mowing the lawn....................$1.00
3. For washing the car....................$ .65
4. For cleaning up his room................$ .50
Total.....................................$2.30

Johnny was a little puzzled when he received no response. But the next morning he understood. Under his plate was a bill: Johnny owes Mother:

1. For cooking his meals......................-0-
2. For cleaning his clothes....................-0-
3. For nursing him night and day when he was sick..-0-
4. For loving and caring for him all his life...........-0-
Total.......................................-0-

Mothers have a wonderful way of imparting true wisdom to each of us. Remember that time when you broke your favorite toy? Mother was there to help you learn that life does not consist in the abundance of toys that a person possesses. Recall that time when you stumbled and fell? The pain seemed so acute! But Mother was there to kiss away the pain and smile away the tears. What about that day when you were disappointed in love? Your favorite chocolate candy seemed bitter! All food formed a boulder in your throat. Everyone appeared to be either snickering behind your back or looking down on this poor, unloved creature—everyone that is, except Mother. Somehow she knew just the words of wisdom that mended your broken heart and changed your mind from the dull gray of despondency into the shamrock green of a smile.

True wisdom is surely one of the blessings for which we

are grateful to our mothers. Secondly, consider the tested instructions about God that we have received from our mothers.

It was Mother who first folded our tiny hands and taught us to pray. Through her we learned that God cares about a little boy who stumps his toe and a little girl who breaks her doll. It was Mother who taught us that wherever we might be, we could talk directly with our Heavenly Father in prayer.

And what a sacred trust is given to every mother to share with her children the tested instruction on how to find Jesus Christ as their personal Savior. It's wonderful when a friend or a Sunday School teacher leads your child to Christ, but it's even more wonderful when a mother shares the good news of Jesus with her child. It is in the home that the child raises his questions about Christ, and it is in the home that the mother is queen. What could be more beautiful or more queenly than for a mother to lead her child to the Master? I recently read again the life of Augustine, the brilliant and saintly bishop of Hippo. One of the secrets of his great life was expressed in this incident: a friend said to Augustine's mother, "Monica, this boy will have to grow up to be a great man because everywhere he walks he will be surrounded by your prayers."

The home is not only the place for instruction and the birth of the Christian life—it is also the place for the nurture of the Christian life. Never be mistaken. A child understands and responds to far more than we realize. When a child commits his life to Christ, he needs the example of his parents to aid him in Christian growth. Faith is a rose that must be guarded and guided with extreme care if it is to bloom into healthy, spiritual maturity. Parents who themselves are devout Christians can guide these young lives in their decisions. They can teach their children the open Bible for Christian commitments and the open mind for spiritual enrichment.

Three blessings we appreciate from our mothers are true wisdom, tested instruction, and tender care. Often, Mother became the willing fingers to prepare a fine meal, to mend some socks, or to bind up an open wound. Many times she brought an attentive ear to listen to our tiniest problems and to let us know that someone was interested, someone cared. It was that wonderful person called Mother who changed our sighs into songs, our jolts into joys, our tragedies into triumphs! No man or woman can be called great who doesn't show his mother that he loves her.

When Garfield was inaugurated as president of the United States, he performed a wonderful service. In the presence of thousands he took his oath of office, but before he delivered his address, he turned and threw his arms around a frail little woman who sat behind him—it was his mother.

When the Spanish-American War was resting heavily upon the shoulders of President McKinley, his mother lay very sick in the old home at Canton, Ohio. He had a private wire from her bedside into the White House and was kept posted every few minutes, night and day. Not knowing what minute they might have to leave, the Pennsylvania Railroad had a train waiting in the depot with the best engine and crew ready for the run.

Over and over the mother kept saying, "Why doesn't William come?" And after a little while, the doctor said, "She is getting worse: you'd better tell him to hurry."

Instantly, the message flashed over the wires and President McKinley sent back the words that are now enshrined in the hearts of the American people: "Tell Mother I'll be there."

Hastily, he jumped on the special train and rushed to Canton. The mayor had halted all traffic, and when the train stopped, the President leaped into a waiting carriage and down the streets they sped on a dead run. Soon they turned the corner by the county courthouse and went east onto Market Street. With a few bounds, he was into the house and into his mother's arms: "Oh, William," she said, "I knew you would make it!"

> As a poor old poet has gently whispered:
> "Don't carve on my tomb any word of fame,
> Or a wheel with the missing spokes,
> Simply let the marble tell my name,
> Then add, "He was good to his folks."

20
The Father's Challenge to Young People
Romans 8:10-15

Did you read where a second-grade boy returned his report card with this admonition: "Teacher, I don't want to scare you or anything like that, but my dad said that if these grades don't start getting better, somebody is going to get a whupping!"

In Italy today you can walk along the Appian Way, the old road from Rome to the provinces over which the chariots of the Caesars rolled in the long ago. There is a segment of this road where it is believed that Simon Peter had a vision of the risen Christ. Somehow we all feel a kindred spirit with Peter because as a young man he was sometimes dedicated, sometimes despondent, like most of us today.

In this case, Peter couldn't get it all together so he was running away, running away from the problems and the persecutions that faced him in Rome. He must have said to himself, "I can do a lot more for the Christian family of the church if I escape this trouble, this tough situation, these formidable enemies in Rome."

Perhaps Peter was rationalizing—it was a normal and natural thing to do. The road to Rome was a rugged road and a rough road.

But this story has an interesting conclusion. As Peter left Rome on the Appian Way and hurried out beyond the borders, the vision of Christ came to check him in his flight. He saw Christ walking back toward Rome!

"Where are you going, Lord?" asked Peter. The Master's

answer was enough to challenge any young person today. "I am going to Rome to be crucified anew." Peter paused, pondered over this challenge, then turned in his tracks, and returned to fight the battle for Christ even in Rome.

A church has been erected on that sight, and today you can visit the church of Quo Vadis. Inside the walls they show you a stone which they believe marks the spot where Jesus stood, and they show you two footprints which they say are the footprints of Jesus.

As you stand in that mystical place, a feeling will sweep gently and movingly through your heart. You will say to yourself, *It doesn't really matter whether these are actually his footprints or not. I only know that sometime ago I dedicated my life to walk in his steps. I must make myself determined enough and honest enough to follow that dedication. I must go on to Rome, my Rome, and give myself afresh to helping Christ build his kingdom right here in this world, right now.*

Each year in the springtime our church has the privilege of sharing in a Youth Week. God, our Heavenly Father, and our earthly parents are genuinely concerned about the sense of dedication and determination of our young people. Several of us technically have passed the student stage of life, and some of us are struggling to start the student stage, but there are several basic principles that make the student's approach most instructive for each member of the family. As students we learn facts, to be sure, but facts in themselves are not the most important part of education. One leading educator today gives this insight: "The most important thing about education is not whether it is content-centered or life-situation centered, whether we learn all the facts or not. The most important thing about an educated person is that he knows where to find the facts and how to interpret them." The emphasis, you see, is not on producing an encyclopedia with hands and feet, a computer in blue jeans and a T-shirt, but on producing a mature, well-balanced, well-adjusted person, a Christian who can cope with life today and perceive eternal consequences. Are you as a young person spiritually alert, spiritually alive, spiritually awake to the spiritual dimensions as well as the horizontal dimensions of life? Are you as a young person committed to Christ, not just for a Sunday religion but for a Monday through Saturday life commitment?

What we need is real dedication to Christ so that the people who know us best and the people who meet us for the first time will recognize that we belong to Christ and Christ belongs to us. Not long ago a speaker raised a question that causes each one of us to reappraise and reevaluate our lives. It was in the context of the martyrs in Europe who were tortured for being Christians, and the speaker raised this penetrating question: "If you today were put on trial for being a Christian, would there be enough evidence to convict you? May I repeat? If you were put on trial for being a Christian, would there be enough evidence to convict you?"

One of the most exciting and enthusiastic fellowships in the Christian family of our church is composed of the young people who come every Thursday night and go visiting for Christ! They offer such realistic, down-to-earth, and genuine prayers. Not long ago, a young person who had just been invited to become a part of this group prayed sincerely, "Thank you, Lord, for helping me to find these Christian young people who have found Christ and who have fun and fellowship with him."

One of the most dynamic Christians of the Middle Ages was Girolamo Savonarola. He shared his faith in Christ with such a contagious enthusiasm that many people reexamined their lives, repented of their sins, and really committed their lives to Christ.

Some of the political powers trumped up false charges against Savonarola and had him burned to death. They led him into the city square, tied him to the stake, bunched up the straw around him, and were about ready to light the torch when they asked him if he had any last words. Savonarola spoke to the glaring crowds of people, "You may burn me alive if you will, but you can never, never, never snatch the living Christ out of my heart!" So saying in genuine dedication, Savonarola sang a little hymn, gazed up into heaven, and went home in triumph to be with God.

Dedication is the first and most important challenge for the young student and the mature Christian, dedication to labor together with God in your own personal Rome, the place of problems, obstacles, and opportunities, and to let God, your Heavenly Father, work through you to build Christ's kingdom into the lives of people.

Then if you have that kind of dedication, you will certainly develop determination. No one will say that the road to learning or the road to Christian maturity is a glistening gateway with no problems and no pains. To imagine that Christian growth is easy and instantaneous is a close encounter of the worst kind. The profound fact is that growth involves struggle and pain. Sometimes the young student has to study when he does not want to study—the subject is dull and drab. Sometimes a mature Christian has to work when he does not want to work—the task is trying and intricate! Christ never looked upon life through rose-colored glasses—he presented a rugged, realistic approach all the way! But always there is that goal just beyond our fingertips, the goal of learning that we might lift other people closer to God our Father, the goal of earning—that we might give sacrifically through the Christian family of the church to provide for people as God provides for people, and the goal of determining that Christ and Christ's service will come first, really first in our lives!

One of the largest oil wells in the world is called Yates Pool in Texas. For years the man who owned the land did not realize its potential worth. He was a sheep rancher and every day he grazed his sheep across the land. His herd grew smaller and smaller. The banker refused to lend him any money to buy any more sheep. He almost lost all he had. One day an exploration company asked permission to drill for oil, and he halfheartedly granted their request.

The first well brought in 80,000 barrels of oil per day. The second well brought in 90,000 barrels of oil per day and has continued to produce for sixteen years! As the man grazed his sheep over that ocean of oil, he lived in poverty! He was a multibillionaire, and he didn't even know it!

In our day—called the aspirin age, the pill paradise, the energy crunch, when people try so hard to forget or to ignore—let us wake up to the fact that we are potentially spiritually richer than we realize! "The earth is the Lord's and the fullness thereof, the world and they that dwell therein."—"The Spirit itself beareth witness with our spirit, that we are the children of God: and if children, then heirs; heirs of God, and joint-heirs with Christ."

If we are dedicated to Christ, and determined to serve as Christ serves, to sacrifice as Christ sacrifices for people, and to share our faith in the living Savior, then we will be excellent students to probe the depths of the riches and wonders of God, mature Christians to cope creatively and successfully with the problems, obstacles, and opportunities of this world in these days! We will make the amazing discovery with the apostle Paul—"I can do all things through Christ which strengtheneth me."

21
Parents' Humble Hearts That Give Love
2 Corinthians 8:3-9

Imagine that the scene is a small village schoolhouse. It is only one week before Christmas and everybody is getting ready for a tremendous celebration. Many of the presents have been bought—the green trees, the holly, and the mistletoe have been gathered from the woods. This afternoon at 2:30 the characters are going to be selected for the Christmas pageant! It must be a great presentation for all the parents will come and the visitors will pack the auditorium.

Excited murmurs have rippled through the young people all morning. Who will get the important parts in the pageant? What girls are really pretty enough to be chosen as angels? Which of the boys look intelligent enough to be Wise Men, or which of the boys are big and strong enough to play the role of the shepherds? Each suggestion raises a nervous snicker and competition is growing keen.

In all the hustle and chatter, there is one character who is lost in the shuffle. Just one person seems so insignificant that no one cares to play his part. Not one single boy wants to be Joseph. He's the man who only stands and gazes at the infant, Jesus, in wonder and adoration and worship. He doesn't get to bring sparkling gifts of gold, frankincense, and myrrh like the Wise Men. He isn't allowed to stride in with a colorful robe and a crooked cane as a glamorous shepherd. Joseph has to just stand with his head bowed and eyes fixed in adoration of Christ, the King.

In our day we sometimes ignore the grace of humility. We become like the sophisticated college sophomore who rewrote the ancient poem to read:

> Twinkle, twinkle, giant star,
> I know exactly what you are,
> An incandescent ball of gas
> Condensing to a solid mass.
>
> Twinkle, twinkle, giant star,
> I need not wonder what you are,
> For seen by spectroscopic ken
> You're helium and hydrogen!

You have to stand in adoration around the cradle of Christ before you can be filled with humility. You have to forget yourself in wonder, like the child whose face really glows when he presses his nose against the store window and gazes at the shiny, new replica of the "Battlestar Galactica." You have to let the might and the majesty and the magnificence of God's gift of love thrill your soul before you can really stand beside the manger and let the Christ warm your heart as he warmed the hearts of those parents of the long ago.

On that star-studded night, Joseph brought his humble homage to Jesus. After he had grown in wisdom and in stature and in favor of God and man, the Son of God said, "If any man will come after me, let him deny himself, and take up his cross, and follow me." The genuine way to let Jesus be born in your heart is to humble yourself and give him your wonder and adoration and worship.

So many people in our day are afraid they will lose their respect and position if they become humble. But this attitude makes you wonder whether they deserve their respect and position. It isn't necessary to barge in and force yourself on people to command their respect. Often you really gain their admiration by being humble.

Ludwig Von Beethoven was one of the greatest musicians that ever lived. After his death, they made his home a shrine in Germany. One day the guide was taking a group of people through the home, and they came to a beautiful piano. The guide would not touch the instrument but quietly nodded as he said, "This piano was the personal instrument of Beethoven."

One woman in the crowd of tourists didn't ask permission. She just waddled over, plopped down on the bench, and played a Beethoven sonata. Then, she looked up with triumph in her eyes, and smiled to the guide, "I suppose you have many people who come to this house and want to play on Beethoven's piano!" But the guide did not smile as he said, "Well, Miss, a few days ago, the greatest living pianist, Paderewski, was here. Many of his friends insisted that he play this instrument, but he refused. Paderewski said, 'Oh, no, I'm not worthy to play on Beethoven's piano!'"

Oh, my friends, when will we learn that people who have true greatness are naturally humble? Today you are invited to humble yourself, like Joseph and Mary, in order to receive the greatest gift you can ever receive, the birth of the Son of God into your heart!

Suppose you had to choose the chief characteristic of Mary, what would you select? A wise choice would be her humility. The angel, Gabriel, brought her incredible news. A virgin to bear a son . . . and that son to be the Son of God . . . both must have seemed impossible to this humble Hebrew maiden.

But notice what happened! Mary did not argue—she did not quibble or debate the matter. She did not even ask for a sign. "And Mary said, Behold, the handmaid of the Lord;

be it unto me according to thy Word" (See Luke 1:38 ff.). A woman who was humble enough to trust the living God!

On that star-sparkling night in the long ago, people brought gifts to the cradle of Christ. The shepherds may have brought a lamb, the angels brought a song of peace, the Wise Men brought gold and frankincense and myrrh. But what could Mary and Joseph bring?

They had come to pay taxes, therefore we know they were out of money. Back in Nazareth they had no palatial houses or rich lands. What did they bring to the Christ child? They brought the requirement that Jesus has always asked—hearts that were worshipful and warm enough to love him for life.

People in our day are concerned with demands. Jesus Christ does not require that you bring him the most elaborate gift you can find, but he does demand something that is your very own. Christ wants you to give something that is not borrowed or handed to you for the purpose of giving. From the young to the old, from the wise to the foolish, from the rich to the poor, the requirement is something that we all can give—a humble heart that truly loves Christ.

The second-grade schoolroom was bustling with activity. This Christmas the children had a new idea. Instead of bringing gifts to put around the Christmas tree and exchange with each other, they had decided to bring clothes to give to the poor. Their teacher had explained that a gift to the poor was a gift to Jesus.

Enthusiasm was mounting higher and higher as the multicolored pile of clothes became a small mountain. But Johnny's parents were just too poor for him to bring anything. Naturally, it seemed to Johnny that everyone had brought a present to give for Jesus but him. After school one day he waited to talk with his teacher. Tears were almost ready to fall as he explained, "Mama and Daddy say we are too poor for me to bring a present for Jesus, but I love him and I want to bring one so much!" "Well," said the teacher, "I gave several sweaters, so we'll just let one of the sweaters be a present from you."

"No," persisted Johnny, "it must be my very own present."

The next day the problem was solved in an unexpected way. Someone brought a pair of shoes that didn't have any shoelaces. Johnny got an idea. Suddenly he sat down on the floor, took out his own shoelaces, and put them in the pair of shoes. "Shucks," said Johnny as he gazed at his love gift for Jesus, "I can use strings!"

Two parents from the long ago ask us a searching question today—Are we humble enough to give unto Christ from hearts of love?

22
The Fires of the Family Altar Kept Aflame
Luke 15:11-18

When the family meets for even a few moments each day to pray together, when the family takes time to open their hearts and minds and souls to the quickening of God's Holy Spirit, then each member of that family will grow in wisdom, statue, and in favor with God and man. Now as never before we need to be deeply concerned about the kind of homes that we build and the kind of families that we produce.

This moving account really has many points to strike home to our intellects and hearts. We often think of Jesus' story of the lost son as being an inspirational message to lead the lost to Christ. It indicates God the Father's love and compassion and concern for people. Let us analyze another insight that Jesus gives us in this story. In effect, Jesus said: "Behold a certain man had two sons. The younger son said to him, 'Dad, the lure of the outside world has captured my imagination. I no longer want to be close to you, I want to be close to the world. Please give me the money you had planned on leaving me as an inheritance, and I'll be shoving off. Those far away places with the strange sounding names are calling. They're calling to me.' The older brother exclaimed in effect, "Dad, give him the money and let him be gone. He's never been very much help to us here in our business anyway. Let's wash our hands of this ungrateful boy and send him away!" With a heavy heart, the father gives to his younger son his inheritance and away the son goes into the far country.

There this young man had all the ingredients to participate in every temptation. He had untested and untried youth; he had abundant money for which he himself had not worked; he had no parents to give him guidance. Like many Americans in this society of today, he was captured by the worship of personal comfort and convenience rather than being recaptured by the worship of his personal God! As you would expect, this young man took the roller-coaster ride to the wreck of his life!

But notice carefully that no matter how far he strayed, that no matter how greatly he sinned, this young man always remembered that he had a father and a family! Jesus used a beautiful and meaningful phrase when he said that after this young man came to himself, he said, "I will arise and go to my father."

The psychiatrists and psychologists and sociologists of our day are reiterating what Jesus taught us hundreds of years ago—that the influence and the inspirations of our homelives stay with us all our lives! Shall we make it ever more pointed and say that the only thing that enabled this young man to come to himself was the fact that he had been reared in a good family with the inspiration and strength of the father and the undergirding and the understanding of the mother. It was the memory, the deeply ingrained memory of the fact that he had wonderful parents and a wonderful Christian family that caused this young man to come to himself and to return to that haven of hope called home.

Oh, how we need to fan the flames of the family altar in our homes today! It is inconceivable and inconsistent and incongruous that any parents should name the name of Jesus and not have a few moments at home to talk about the great Shepherd and Savior and King, and to talk to God as revealed to us in this Christ Jesus!

Often parents today wait until their children are eighteen or nineteen years old, and then, they begin to worry about their children. Perhaps the child has gone out for the evening and the parents pace the floor. It's late—it's dark, they don't know exactly where that child is, and the parents are overwhelmed with concern. The Bible tells us to "train up a child in the way he should go: and when he is old, he will not depart from it." When a child gets to be eighteen or nineteen years old, his Christian insights and principles and standards, or lack of them, are fairly well formed. From the first moment that a Christian man and a Christian woman are united in the sacred bonds of marriage, they need the family altar! Even the baby needs to see his parents read the Word of God and share in prayers in his home. One of the greatest teachers of Christian morals that Southern Baptists have ever had was Dr. O. T. Binkley who declared in a class one morning, "The child is capable of religious feeling long before he is capable of religious thought."

Parents today are so concerned about giving their children lessons in horseback riding, canoeing, piano,—parents must not, dare not, neglect giving their children lessons in prayer in the homes!

Come, my friend, and let us reason together. The Bible calls upon us to have faith. Do you believe that the people of our church and our city can have a sense of purpose in their lives that will carry them through the darkest dungeons of gloom and despair? Do you believe that the people of our fellowship can have a source of strength that will make them more than conquerors of any and every adversary? It may sound impossible, but it is absolutely reasonable and redemptive and necessary! We can have it, we can achieve it, if parents will covenant personally with Christ that they will take the initiative, that they will make the effort, and that they will take the time to talk about Jesus and to talk to Jesus in prayer in their home every day! Someone has well said that a home is a roof to keep out the rain, four walls to keep out the wind, and floors to keep out the cold—but a home is much more than that! A home is the smile of the child, the song of the mother, the strength of the father, and the creative place where Christ is a welcome friend and guest. A home without a family altar is like a house without a roof—there is no protection from the storms of life. We must covenant personally with God to make the effort and take the time to fan the holy flames of the family altar in our homes.

The late, great George W. Truett was preaching one evening on the family altar and pleading with the people to put first things first, asking the men who were Christians to pause at the breakfast table for a season of prayer with the loved ones around them, or pause in the evening time, gather the family together, and speak about the Savior. Many people came by and resolved to have a family altar in their homes. One outstanding businessman, whose voice was heard often in the city, said, "Pastor, I've lived miserably far from what is right and consistent. Family prayer shall be at my house tonight and every night from this day on!"

The next morning as the pastor was riding across the city, he saw this man's sixteen-year-old son standing at the corner and the boy summoned him to stop. The boy's face revealed an intense battle going on, and the pastor said, "What is it, my friend? How can I help you?" The boy looked down at his feet and looked up with a face covered with tears as he said, "You ought to have been at our house last night."

"What happened at your house, my friend? I would like to know." The boy continued, "Oh, you should have been there! Daddy prayed last night! Daddy had Sister and me called into the room, and he sobbed as he told us he had not lived like a Christian father ought to live, and he asked Sister and me to forgive him. Neither one of us could say anything. We didn't know what to say. We just cried with him. Daddy asked Mother to open the Bible for him and he read a few verses, then he knelt down and prayed, mostly about himself and our family. When he arose, he said, 'Children, Dad is going to live a different life, from now on we are going to have the family prayer time in our home.'"

The boy explained, "I went up to my room but I couldn't go to sleep. I realized last night that I'm not a Christian and I wanted to see you this morning that you might help me find Christ."

The pastor turned the car off the busy street, and there after a few words, the boy found Jesus as his Savior and began to walk in the magnificent sunlight of Christ's love.

The next Sunday morning, when the invitation was given, that boy led the way. He stepped out from his pew and walked down the aisle triumphantly and openly giving his life to Christ. As they stood at the front of the congregation, the pastor said, "Tell us, my boy, what started you on the upward way toward Christ?" The boy looked across the vast congregation and straight into the eyes of his father as he said simply, "It was Dad's prayer—it was Dad's prayer last Sunday night at home that started me on the upward way to Christ!"